Dendrophilia and Other Social Taboos: True Stories

Dani Burlison

Dendrophilia and Other Social Taboos: True Stories

© 2013 Dani Burlison

Published by Petals & Bones Press

Digital version available at www.ebookpie.com

First Edition, First Printing: December 2013

ISBN: 978-0-615-92827-2

Cover Design: Josh Staples at Headlong Into Harm

Interior Layout: Will McCollum

Printed by Blurb

www.blurb.com

Most of this collection was first published at **McSweeney's Internet Tendency,**
September 2011 - September 2012.

Other stories appeared in the following publications (and are reprinted here with
permission from editors):

Don't Touch Me There, **North Bay Bohemian,** February 2010.
Buying Time first appeared in the Sex Issue of **Rad Dad Zine,** August 2010

and also ran in **Offbeat Mama,** April 2011.
Stop Making Sense, **The Pacific Sun,** September 2011.

Petals and Bones Press

Part 1. These Kinds of Things

1. Don't Touch Me There

2. It's Not Cannibalism If Nobody Died

3. I Feel Hurt When You Are An Asshole

4. Spiritually Cleansing Naked Places: Some Insider Advice

5. Rejected Travel Magazine Query: Sex Tourism On A Budget

6. Eminem Sex Dreams Decoded

7. Stop Making Sense

8. DIY Ecstatic Dance Jam

Part 2. Other Kinds of Things

9. The Geography Of Uncool: Public Transportation

10. Hired Help

11. Pasty Little Inner Mutt

12. Go Big, Go Redwood: An Arbor Day Love Story

13. Bad Feminist

14. Buying Time

15. One Settled Comfortably In The Cukoo's Nest

16. I'm Dreaming Of An Anne Frank Christmas

17. If You Like Piña Coladas

18. Like A Born-Again Almost 40-Year-Old Virgin

19. Katie The Tarot Whisperer

For Xenia & Ava,

Thank you for the endless material... I adore you.

Part 1:

These Kinds of Things

Don't Touch Me There

"I don't know if they have Valium at Target, but I will check," read the text message. My friend Skye was at the store in search of a matching set of footie pajamas for us. "This is it," I thought to myself as beads of sweat formed across my forehead. "We are actually going to a fucking cuddle party."

I first heard of cuddle parties from a friend who planned one as her divorce steadily approached finalization. "Apparently, it is a safe place to explore nonsexual touch," she told me optimistically. I found myself both intrigued and curiously disgusted as she explained the concept: a group of strangers come together in a safe space to give and receive affection. Perhaps this could be the next step in my life as an armchair anthropologist, a practice in furthering my experience in field research and an opportunity to test my own boundaries and practice saying no. But stepping into an environment so far out of my comfort zone that I might as well be visiting Pluto was also a little horrifying. I needed some reassurance.

The information on the front page of the CuddleParty.com website is straightforward and nonthreatening. Yet I couldn't erase the visions in my mind of middle-aged pony-tailed dudes cruising for young, pretty, affirmation-thumping New Age women. As I poked around the internet, however, photos of past parties, revealing bare arms intertwining indistinguishably in a sea of flannel-pajama bottoms and overstuffed pillows, tapped into a deep fear inside of me. Thoughts of germs and cold, clammy hands running lightly across my back while moaning and sighing mixed with enchanted dolphin music invoked visions of what I imagined would be not unlike an unwilling visit to a couple's tantra retreat. My blood pressure rose. I laughed nervously. I decided that I needed to go and see for myself.

As we drove the streets of San Francisco, Skye already sporting his completely awesome glow-in-the-dark footie pajamas, I prayed that we would be lost for so long that they would not admit our late arrival. Being one of the most grounded and open-minded of my friends, Skye was there to calm my nerves and talk me down from the extreme anxiety I was experiencing.

"I bet you 20 bucks that there are silk scarves and batik sarongs on the ceiling," I giggled to him as we arrived at our destination. We climbed the stairs and I took one last deep breath before marching up to introduce ourselves in the futon-filled room and pay the $30 per-person entrance fee. I looked up. Scarves and sarongs draped the ceiling.

As I slinked down the dark hallway to change into my pajamas, a tall, lanky man dressed in a purple satin wraparound blouse, white short-shorts and purple opaque tights approached me. He stood against my slight frame with his hand on his hip and asked if this was my first cuddle party. "Do you get an edge from this kind of thing?" he asked. "I mean, like, do you really get an edge from this?"

I replied that it was my first cuddle party, embarrassed to admit that I had no idea what "edge" meant. We chatted for a few minutes, and I decided that this guy, who was flamboyantly gay and presumably not interested in women and therefore nonthreatening, would be my new pal, my Safe Buddy, so to speak. A sigh of relief escaped while imagining my new friend and I sitting back and chatting about the silliness of the whole situation.

I slipped into the bathroom and emerged a new woman–Dani, champion of the cuddle party–dressed quite literally from head to toe in a set of boy's dark-blue footie pajamas, decorated with rocket ships and glow-in-the-dark stars. Skye and I matched perfectly, and as we entered the cuddle room, we were happily greeted by 20 other guests who were sitting haphazardly in a circle on a makeshift, pillow-laden bed.

We began with introductions and a brief history of cuddle parties, before continuing on to rules. Despite my original assumption that cuddle parties arose from a West Coast commune after residents ingested one too many psychedelic mushroom caps, the parties actually originated on the East Coast. Founded in 2004 in New York by relationship coaches Reid Mihalko and Marcia Baczynski as a place for people of all genders and walks of life to explore touch in a safe, sober and structured environment, cuddle parties have gained popularity around the globe.

There are several rules which include keeping clothing on at all times, being completely alcohol and drug-free and only making physical contact after receiving a verbal yes to a specific and clear request to touch. There are also "cuddle lifeguards," who are trained co-facilitators placed onsite to ensure that everyone is comfortable and safe.

After I'd recovered from the shock of discovering that kissing, groping and erections were all acceptable at the party, we quickly moved on to boundary-setting exercises, which revived my confidence and led me to practice giving an abundance of verbal no's. I proceeded to glide back and forth through the crowded room in my celestial jammies, repeating "No" over and over to nearly everyone in the room and their requests to touch, kiss or otherwise fondle me. I felt empowered, like I was sporting an invisible cape and shield to detour any unwanted advances with pride and dignity.

This empowerment came to a screeching halt when, after a man in his late 50s excitedly shared that he had no touch boundaries and liked to be touched "in any way, by any one, at any time," the facilitators asked the attendees to drop to all fours and begin crawling around the room like "magical cows in a mystical forest."

As if things weren't awkward enough with a bunch of adults sitting around some random living room in pajamas, completely stone cold sober on a Sunday afternoon, now we had to act like cows, crawling around and mooing like idiots. I understood this to be an ice-breaking exercise to lead us into the next stage of the three-and-a-half-hour-long touch-fest, but all I wanted to break were my legs so Skye could quickly rush me out of the room and to the nearest hospital before anyone could touch me. But before I could crawl through the crowd to make a break for it, the cows had tipped to their sides and begun to cuddle.

I have had my fair share of physical and emotional intimacy. I have stumbled into intriguing and boundary-testing situations in places like Burning Man, yoga retreats, cocktail parties and even once at a Super Bowl party in my own living room. I have been strewn across a mattress in the "chill room" of a 1990s rave with complete strangers massaging my every muscle while I puffed away on menthol cigarettes. What sets these incidents apart from the format of a cuddle party is the lack of expectation, formal structure and, of course, the buffer of controlled substances. Entirely sober and surrounded by strangers, I couldn't read their minds and had no way of knowing if the generous offers of hand-holding held deeper intentions.

I made for the bathroom, tripping over a penis pillow on the way and rummaging through my bag for the last time in hopes of discovering one last overlooked Xanax before I sucked it up, accepted my fate and returned to poor, dear Skye, who had managed to cram his body, in full fetal position, into the smallest corner of the room. If my body language was saying "Please don't touch me," Skye's read more like a serial killer ready to pull a chainsaw on the first person to even look at him. His open mind seemed to have gone on strike. I squeezed into the corner with him, observing the active and diverse scene.

Young polyamorous couples took turns caressing the hair of those next to them. A middle-aged, six-foot-tall transgendered woman tangled herself up in the arms of a young, attractive South Asian immigrant man whose hands were groping the breasts of a thirty-something yoga instructor. And just when I grew comfortable enough to accept an offer of a foot rub from a married cuddle-party frequenter, I noticed my Safe Buddy, Mr. Purple Pants, groping and grinding a woman while they twisted their tongues in a fit of exhibitionist passion. (Apparently, I missed the "rule" stating that kissing, dry- humping and rubbing genitals are not sexual touch.)

One of the rules did mention that attendees could get up and walk out at any time, but I was honestly too worried about calling attention to myself. I suddenly felt old-fashioned, boring and old. I just couldn't let go of my inhibitions like everyone else in the room. I felt an almost palpable wall building itself up around me as the partygoers continued to push their boundaries by allowing stranger's hands to wander and rub and caress in the most interesting ways. I was freaked and continued to nervously laugh and chat with anyone in the room who looked as horrified as I until an announcement came that the party was winding down.

The facilitator invited everyone to join in for one last hurrah by piling up into a giant "cuddle puddle" for the remaining 20 minutes of the party. As Skye stood, paralyzed by the scene that played out before him, I made one last ditch effort to open my mind. I crawled around the circle and was invited to lay my head on the shoulder of the young South Asian man in the gender-bending three-way. I accepted and placed my head on his shoulder with my entire body on the outside of the circle, cold and constricted like an armadillo under attack. I attempted to relax into the moment. Relaxation never came.

As we laughed and recapped the experience on our drive home, I realized that I had learned something fairly valuable during that party. While cuddle parties certainly provide the benefits of physical touch for those who may not regularly have access to affection for various reasons, I felt that this particular party was no more a practice in intimacy than the husband who refuses to be affectionate or sexual with his wife, yet forks over cash for sex or is otherwise promiscuous with strangers.

The experience also confirmed in me that when it comes to affection and intimacy, I am indeed old-fashioned. I desire that sense of safety and closeness that comes from sustained relationships built on trust. And I will certainly never be attending a cuddle party again–at least, not without some hand-sanitizer and Valium on hand.

It's Not Cannibalism if Nobody Died

Recently, a close friend got knocked up. The reality of how pregnancy changes lives brought with it trepidation, excitement and many sleepless nights.

In the latter months of her pregnancy, she joined me for tea and conversation. As an experienced mother (i.e. a single mom with one kid having survived thus far into teenagerdom and another trailing closely behind), friends approach me with inquiries about the perils and triumphs of parenting. Often the questions resemble the following: "How do I know if my wife's breast milk is heated enough for the baby?" Or "Did you have hemorrhoids all up in your business when you were preggo?" Or even "Man, did you want to screw everything in your third trimester or WHAT?" On this particular day of tea and talk, the conversation unfolded like this:

FRIEND: I am worried about postpartum depression.

ME: You should be. That shit is serious. I fantasized about killing both of my kids and myself every day after my second was born.

FRIEND: Whoa. So, will you prepare my placenta so I don't lose my mind after the baby is born?

ME: Uh, ok.

I should be clear here. My friend was not desiring a meal and did not ask me to boil her up some **polenta** with gruyère, sea salt and a side of garlic-sauteed collard greens. She asked me to take her afterbirth into my kitchen and do all sorts of things to it in hopes of preventing postpartum depression. And I said yes. Not because processing her afterbirth was the best invitation I was offered at the time, but because I live in Sonoma County and that's the kind of thing we do up here. Also, anything that keeps a lady friend from going ape shit crazy on her baby or herself is okay by me.

Now, many of us have sat patiently by while new parents share sweet tales of burying a firstborn child's placenta under an apple tree in a backyard or driving it to a favorite wilderness destination to release it as an offering to the baby-loving gods. But most stories involving the consumption of this surprisingly large, kidney-looking organ include wild animals–not humans–who suck amniotic fluid from their freshly born offspring's pelt before gobbling down the placenta and umbilical cord for nutrition.

Of course it sounds unappetizing. Absolutely. It's a giant blood clot, after all. But think about it: If each person held within them a potential remedy for agonizing mental health issues, wouldn't we all be getting all over it, bringing forth our insides like a glob of magical super blue-green algae from the fountain of youth, before stuffing it back down our gullets? I was mostly vegan at the time of my own wretched baby- accompanied lunacy, but if I was told that eating my own afterbirth would have prevented me from holing up behind shuttered windows, weeping all night with my colic-stricken baby and resorting to an emotional email affair based on a shared and shameful love of **Temptation Island** episodes, I would have popped a straw into that sucker like a fresh equatorial coconut and slurped until its bloody essence filled my weary soul.

Naturally, I offered my friend unwavering support.

With the anticipated arrival of her baby and accompanying giant natural mental health booster it was attached to, I found myself embarking on an exciting new research project. Though somewhat familiar with the idea that the hormones contained in the pulpy mass may assist in balancing the new mother's hormones and assist in lactation and mood stabilization, I soon learned many facts about Placentophagy, or, eating afterbirth. The placenta contains protein, iron and hormones that also assist in post-birth contractions, which in turn help deliver that stretched out uterus to pre-baby size. But what was I supposed to do with it once I got it in my kitchen?

I consulted an acupuncturist and Chinese herbalist friend and received some recipes for processing the bloody mess into a palatable concoction; a dried herbal supplement, Ziheche. I often dabbled in herbal medicine making and spent my childhood peering into the family room while my brothers skinned raccoons, muskrats and foxes for fur trade shows. Surely drawing from these experiences would help me manifest the wisdom and appropriate cutlery skills needed to proceed with determination.

Months later, as I waited by the door, flip-flopping between confidence and uncertainty, I did my best to channel Angelica Houston's made-for-tv priestess role as Lady of the Lake in HBO's rendition of *The Mists of Avalon.* It was a Sunday evening in April and the door creaked open with a burst of spring air. The big day had arrived. My friend and her husband found themselves parents of a darling Kewpie Doll look-alike. I found myself opening the door to the baby's aunt and a cooler packed with ice and a not-so-darling chunk of afterbirth.

"I feel like we're doing a drug deal or black market kidney trade or something," she said as she handed it over.

"We sort of are," I replied with mixed feelings about the Igloo cooler's freshly harvested contents.

I decided that if I filled the house with music from Loreena McKennitt the whole process would become spiritually fulfilling. Enlightening, even. But the songs just bothered me. I switched gears and threw on something more appropriate for the occasion, knowing that my friend would appreciate the infusion of Nick Cave's energy into her Ancient Chinese Secret.

I draped myself in a flattering vintage apron, snapped on the rubber surgical gloves left over from my teenage daughter's last bad hair dye job and went for it.

I opened the cooler, feeling brave and righteous and like the most supportive friend ever in the history of the entire universe. There it sat, a giant blob encased in a large freezer-sized Ziploc. My surgical-glove-covered hands dove in past the blue ice packs and in my mind the mass transitioned from uterine glob to a plastic-wrapped science experiment flopping into a copper colander.

As I unwrapped the baby steak, I found my gag reflex fighting against the DIY feminist healer inside and all instincts tugged at me to throw the thing out the window. Or feed it to my cat. Still, I resisted, blasting water from the faucet in order to rinse out excess blood before sawing at the amniotic sac and gristly umbilical cord. As I freed the organ from any non-placenta attachments, I mustered the will to halt any thoughts of this fleshy red object as "my friend's giant period."

After rinsing, the placenta was transported to a mechanism on the stovetop, where rice wine vinegar warmed, providing a slow, painfully long steaming session. During this step in the process, hormones released into the air like a whirling magic entity of pungent, odorous womanhood, serving as a dude repellant while simultaneously attracting sexually frustrated and hungry creatures, both wild and domestic.

After several hours, the partially cooked and now gray meat was carefully moved to a cutting board where I proceeded to chop it into stew-sized niblets before it retired to a food dehydrator for the evening.

The following morning, the house was aired out for fear that the thick hormone vapor that hung like sauna steam in a filthy happy ending spa would cause me to lactate, lose my libido, or worse. I brewed up some coffee, washed out the grinder and clunked the dried chunks of placenta in, one by one. After soliciting the help of my totally grossed out teenager, the cayenne-looking powder that resulted was packed into capsules.

ME: Honey, can you help me put this placenta into these capsules?

TEENAGER: Mom, that is gross. And I'm a vegetarian and this is, like, cannibalism or something.

ME: Come on! It's hardcore! Besides, it's not cannibalism if nobody died!

Our bodies are impossibly complex mechanical creatures with constantly evolving, phenomenal activity. Bodily functions are incredible. Giving birth is amazing. Miraculous, even. But pregnancy and childbirth certainly aren't "beautiful" like so many woo-woos claim. There are rips and screams and tears and fountains of putrid juices including, on occasion, obscene amounts of blood, urine, vomit, slime colored amniotic fluid and even varying amounts of fecal matter. And the placenta, although fascinating when really seriously contemplated and appreciated for all it does to keep mom and baby connected for nine months is still inarguably one of the most unsightly specimens to cradle in one's hands.

As far as the friend who ingested her own highly processed afterbirth, her milk gushed out in gallons.

FRIEND: Dude, Dani. I almost drown my baby every day because I am lactating so much. It's crazy.

ME: At least you aren't drowning her in the bathtub because a little postpartum voice told you to.

FRIEND: True that.

I Feel Hurt When You Are An Asshole

Under normal circumstances, I fully encourage and support any attempt one makes to improve interpersonal communication. Especially when it benefits me.

A partner using "I" statements and engaging in concerted efforts to be clear, open and honest warms my heart. A boss or coworker that communicates clear guidelines and expectations is a cherished gem that I would regularly polish if not for pesky sexual harassment laws. Children that are able to clearly state what is or isn't working in regards to my half-ass attempts at helping with homework make it easier for me to justify hiring a tutor. I love boundaries. I relish opportunities to really, deeply understand what someone needs or how they feel. It is a wonderful feeling to know that I am surrounded–for the most part–by people that are not assholes and know how to communicate.

Unfortunately, there are people in this world that believe–deep down in their indigo-shaded tie-dyed souls–that they are effective communicators. What these people don't realize is that they are crazy.

Take wannabe Nonviolent Communication devotees, for instance. And also, people who are sociopaths.

The premise seems harmless enough: Nonviolent Communication is a self-righteous cult-like language style that supposedly facilitates the flow of communication needed to exchange information and resolve differences peacefully. It also claims to help focus attention on compassion as a motivating factor, instead of guilt, blame, fear or shame. In some cases, it helps people to own their feelings. This, I appreciate. I always own the shit out of my feelings, and sometimes everyone else's feelings, too. Growing up in an obscenely large dysfunctional family molded me into a loyal codependent. Thanks, Mom and Dad!

The framework of Nonviolent Communication adds a lot of unnecessary words to sentences, though, and can chew up anywhere from four to thirty-five minutes of any given day. For example, if someone doesn't feel like going on a date with the drunk woman that accosted them in their therapist's parking lot, they can just give a calm and brief "no, thanks" as a reply to the solicitation. Or utilize the pepper spray tucked away in their bicycle's panniers. In Nonviolent Communication Fantasy Land, the response would be more like this: "I feel uncomfortable with the level of your alcohol intake and I am needing to stay home and watch the ***Deadliest Catch*** marathon this weekend." The latter statement sets a revolving door of interaction into motion and invites questions. And questions always lead to conversation. It seems to complicate things. And it wastes a lot of precious time. Thirty-five minutes a day means about eight days out of an entire year used to engage in conversations with people we'd rather avoid when we could be doing something fun like sleeping. Or planting five acres of corn. Or having oral surgery.

In almost every instance, if the feelings bubbling up from our instinctive cores incite feelings of aversion, it is quite alright to say, "no." Take this woman I knew who, loyal to her Nonviolent Communication teachings, decided it was appropriate to "honor" her two-year-old's needs to repeatedly not get dressed in the morning. In typical terrible-twos fashion, he screamed and cried while he ran amok, tearing their apartment to shreds; his need for control running the game. The mother listened calmly and replied, "I hear that you are not wanting to get dressed right now, Lil Johnny. I honor your feelings and we can try again later."

This is crazy talk.

A two-year-old doesn't even know it has needs, nor does it recognize what those needs are beyond hunger or the deep desire to covet its sibling's Playmobil pirate ship. An appropriate response would have been to lasso that little bastard and shove him into a heavily starched straightjacket and get on with the Goddamn day. Next, this woman is completely oblivious to the fact that she is raising one of many in a generation of monsters.

This little asshole will grow up to be a large, adult-sized asshole who will eventually enter the workforce and begin relationships. Without a serious emotional smack down and some mild shaming once in a while, kids like this become men and women with no sense of personal boundaries, frequently displaying asshole behavior because they "feel like it." Also, the world is a cruel, gruesome place full of unanticipated pain and we should all be prepared for the hands of life shoving us down dark stairwells of disappointment every chance it gets.

In the worst case scenario of overly permissive, pot-smoking new-age parenting gone horribly, horribly awry, Lil Johnny will grow up to ruin the lives of women everywhere. He will pose as a Middle Eastern James Franco and stalk his ex-girlfriends on OKCupid because doing so meets his need of feeling in control. He will also hack into an ex-girlfriend's email and sneak into her house to snoop through her things, opting to remove items that he feels she no longer needs because no one told him not to do it. Since she left her door unlocked, he'll argue that he did nothing wrong. And he'll expect everyone to honor his feelings as he walks away with his arms full of her brand new size 34B bra and panty sets along with her self- help books on verbally abusive relationships.

The rationalization for some of his displays of other wildly inappropriate behavior will surely include passive-aggressive word play: "I am sorry your anxiety causes you to choose to perceive me as a bad person because I got drunk, called you a slut and left drunk in the middle of the night to make plans to screw my ex-girlfriend. Maybe you should think long and hard about what you did to make me need to do that."

It's enough to make even the most sane person want to rip their veins out through their eye sockets in fits of unbearable confusion.

It doesn't end with a few cases of Lil Johnny Lacks Boundaries. I believe that Nonviolent Communicator wannabes are the foulest creatures to walk among us. Most blend in and appear to be every day, normal people who frequent parks, bookstores, cafes, independent movie theaters and live music venues. Most of them are upper-middle-class white folks who drive Priuses or Subaru Outbacks slathered with bumper stickers reading "One Love" or "Inquire Within." Upon close inspection, they can be spotted by an air of narcissism swirling around them and eyes that are open just wide enough to see the white orb curving back above their irises. They never blink. They carelessly block the gourmet cheese aisle at the neighborhood co-op. Often, while pretending to listen with an open heart chakra, their heads tilt just slightly to the right, as if positioning the left ear a few centimeters toward an open mouth will help them hear more fully. If they are in agreement with what they hear, their eyes squint and their heads will begin to bob like they are grooving to an inner rhythm of a slow-jam-meets-smooth-jazz-remix of Terrence Trent D'Arby. Or like their ecstasy just started kicking in and they are remembering the strawberry lollipop they stashed in the freezer. They moan and sigh a lot when a phrase moves them. Also, some of them are mouth breathers.

Sometimes, they will adorn themselves with one or more wardrobe items–earrings, a swath of sustainably harvested, fair trade berry-died alpaca fabric holding locks of hair in place or even a wallet or purse–that appears "ethnic" or "multicultural" as if wearing a Guatemalan print vest makes them a legitimate expert on socially acceptable behavior or proactive communication techniques. (Side-note: Unless the person wearing this type of garb actually lives in a developing country and is the village medicine man or woman, they should never be taken seriously. Ever. Walk away.)

These people meet in groups to practice not being assholes, or, giving empathy as described in a group that my friend Henry and I crashed last week before drinking off the panic attacks the meeting created. Correction: we met our needs of wanting calmness by drinking beer and trying to make sense of the new lingo we encountered. Apparently, acting like a giraffe is good but being a Jackal is bad. What about meerkats or aardvarks, we wondered. The club seems so exclusive and discriminatory.

But it isn't merely the aesthetics of unfortunate fashion choices or the superiority complex that shines through their eyes to the condescending tone residing deep in their solar plexuses that makes these people some of the most irritating humans to be cornered by at a vegan cocktail party. Some of them may have heartfelt intentions of making the world a better place. To them I say, Kumbaya, My Lord. Still, there is a fine line between Nonviolent Communication and verbal manipulation. Speaking in a calm, clear tone makes no difference if what you are saying is abusive, just plain stupid or meant to make someone hate herself in order for you to get what you want.

Nonviolent Communication tactics may be perfectly appropriate in circles of self-righteous, passive aggressive cultish circles or among people who are independently wealthy, leaving them with endless hours to devote to self-improvement gimmicks. It leaves the rest of us exposed to the bitter wind of impatience and unanswered questions. And quite frankly, it transforms otherwise normal and understanding people into a pack of angry, mangy wolves. I wish people could just be decent.

But these are just my feelings.

I still have a preference for a "yes" or "no" over some long-winded inconclusive response from some creep whose prolonged eye contact makes me want an Ambien.

Obviously I need to look at the "needs list" in Chapter 5 of my Nonviolent Communication book and reflect on what is missing in my life.

I think I just feel hurt when people act like assholes and I need them to go away and never talk to me ever again.

Maybe I just need some empathy. Or maybe people should just try harder to stop being assholes.

Spiritually Cleansing Naked Places

So you've been stressed. You need a vacation. The nagging tendonitis from hours of editing your unpublishable manuscript has left you frustrated, tense. A friend suggests you join her for a day trip to the semi-local Hot Springs resort. You can't drink there, but you can get a massage and soak your aching, overworked body in hot mineral water while surrounded on all sides by rolling hills and wildlife and fresh air and naked men. Here are some crucial insider tips for making the most of your experience:

Wear a humongous low-rimmed **sun hat.** This will not only protect your eyes from solar flares and shield your scalp and forehead from damaging UV rays, but it will also serve as a buffer. The larger the hat, the darker the shadow it casts across your face. This will be useful in concealing the stunned and mangled expressions your face will likely display during your visit. And unless you have very identifiable body art, the hat will also ensure that your child's former preschool teacher won't recognize you and stop by to show you her new lowerback Luna Moth tattoo.

Always wear big, **dark sunglasses.** Again, the sun is bright out there in the wild, wild world of naked hot springs. You need protection. You also need those glasses to shield your delicate eyes from so many unwanted soul stares that are guaranteed while visiting the magic crystal lands of spiritually cleansing naked places. They also serve as a softening screen when presented with the many, many pale white asses and tenderly scalded crispy pink buns that come frighteningly close to your face. Bonus: Dark glasses make it possible for you to ogle the rare attractive man or woman lounging near the pool without looking like a total perv.

It is very important to utilize the most basic of manners at the hot springs, like "no peeing in the pool" and "ladies first." But most importantly, ***remember not to bend over*** to pick up your book bag or vegan chocolate treats. And don't attend any yoga classes sans pants. You wouldn't like someone else's puckered starfish or withering junk dangling in your face, would you? Just kneel. Better yet, if you're hoping to make a few naked friends during your visit, ask someone at ground level to assist you in retrieving your items.

Another important tip is to be aware of the ***personal space*** of others and yourself and don't–for any reason–pass through (or even come within three feet of) circles of fellow hot springs seekers. People who form into naked body mandala clusters are often working out some Aura wounds or practicing some sort of hocus pocus. If you enter into the sacred geometric space they've formed, the possibility of being sucked into an accidental energetic Ménage à hecka or of having your qi altered into an unmanageable state of disarray increases tenfold. Unprotected psychic energy field swaps can be avoided. Just stay away.

Massages at places where most people are unclothed and so god damn spiritual can be hit or miss, so opt for a deep tissue massage in lieu of a discounted warm Himalayan rock salt chakra balancing energy work treatment. Even expressing a desire for something soothing like a basic Swedish Massage can misinterpreted, providing the body worker an opportunity to process some psychic issues around unbalanced menstrual cycles or grief over the dead ladybug they found in their raw kale salad the week before. If you're not careful about who is selected to administer these often pricey hour-long treatments, you may very well end up alone in a room with someone who provides little more than uncomfortably loud rhythmic breathing and low-grade humming noises while they criticize you for being too tense and not joining their primitive harmonics.

It is easy to notice a lot of unsuppressed and even aggressive **moaning and sighing** when everyone around you is naked. People are fucking STOKED to walk around naked, dipping in and out of hot and cold and lukewarm water while pretty girls lounge and feed each other organic mangoes and comb their long golden locks just inches above their perky sun-kissed breasts. So lots of old dudes moan. And sigh. Loudly. With every inhalation, with every filling of their stainless steel water bottles, they groan. Don't be alarmed. Don't make eye contact. They're just stoked. No need to moan back.

Don't let anyone but your friend apply your sunblock.

Strangers will appear to be very kind, helpful and even self-less. But it is wise to leave the hard-to-reach-places sunblock application to a trusted friend. There's no telling where the supposed kind hands of strangers may wander to. Sure, the signs say NO SEXUAL CONTACT, but not all of the signs are visible, if you know what I mean.

There is an odd slapping or clapping sound that often drifts through the air on particularly crowded afternoons at the naked hot springs resort. Whatever you do, don't seek its origin, no matter how the curiosity grips you and attempts to force your head in the direction of said sound. The source of the smacking is **the elusive weiner-flapper** and no one needs to see him, ever. Take it from me, one way to ruin any chance of an enjoyable naked hot springs experience is to come face to face with a Gallagher look-alike playing a solo game of penis ping pong with his sunburnt inner thighs.

If there is a hose-like contraption in the **sauna,** give the seating area a good, hard spray before sitting down. I shouldn't need to tell you why.

Once in a while, someone will approach, sparking a light conversation with comments like *It sure is a lovely day, isn't it?* Or: *What does that tattoo signify?* Or: *That raw coconut water is SO REFRESHING* (usually followed by a long moan or sigh). And at some point an offer will come seemingly out of the stranger's overly sun-drenched ass: *Would you like me to float you?* Now, this man may or may not believe he is a wizard with levitation powers but what he is offering doesn't consist of a grown up round of *light as a feather, stiff as a board.* He wants to lead you into the water, where he will do an under water baptism dealio resembling a solo park side tai chi or interpretive dance meets magic trick maneuver while you lie, relaxing in the water, hoping not to drown. It looks whimsical and harmless enough but I can't help but think that half of the floatees are held in the water by creepy old man erectile implants.

Don't go to the naked Hot Springs Resort with a hangover. Seriously. Some well-meaning healer will misinterpret your hung-over energy as a major illness or trauma and will try to fix you up good. And by "fix you up good," I mean touch you or get you to engage in the synchronistic sighing that so many naked hot springs resort people are into. And with a looming hangover, you'll be too out of sorts to ask them to stop. Next thing you know, you'll be draped in purple batik sarongs and spread out on the floor of a Nag Champa scented space dome. And everyone knows that kind of thing never ends with a smile. Ever.

And finally, the best and most crucial tip to enjoying the naked hot springs resort is to *stay home* and take a nice hot bath alone instead.

Rejected Travel Magazine Query:
Sex Tourism on a Budget

Dear Fancy Travel Magazine Editor,

I really appreciated the perspective offered in the "Top Ten Pampering Vacations for Women" piece you ran in last month's issue about women and solo travel. The accompanying sidebar on single-occupancy budget hotels under $800 a night really shed a light on how desperately women need to take time to rejuvenate and replenish our overworked lives with a little "me" time. I'm thrilled to learn that hotels like those you often mention in your publication have lowered their costs in response to a growing population of stressed-out single women.

As an experienced solo traveler and freelance writer, I would love an opportunity to contribute a story, "Sex Tourism on a Budget," which is specifically geared toward women in the lower-income brackets of your readership. I think you'd agree that sex tourism is a growing industry with potential to change the world economy while simultaneously eradicating anxiety and depression.

For many of America's eight-hundred billion heterosexual, single, moderate income women in their thirties and forties, the idea of competing for bed time with the twenty-five semi-eligible bachelors currently residing in the Continental United States is as appealing as cashing in Groupons for colon hydrotherapy singles mixers. Most of us opt out of said group colonic treatments, stay home and masturbate to reruns of Anthony Bourdain's *No Reservations* instead of suffering the humiliation of revealing oneself as one more god damn lonely single woman wading through a sea of perky twenty- somethings, blond hair extensions and knee-deep desperation in search of just a moment's worth of eye contact, a prolonged handshake or even an elbow in the rib at these crowded, miserable events.

For one, it's a losing battle. The available woman-to-man ratio is obviously tilted quite heavily in favor of the twenty-five men I mentioned. Women are left competing against one another in ways that even a crank-addicted heavyweight female wrestler would find appalling. After spending thousands of dollars on diets, cosmetic surgery, beauty products and "find your lost and confused soul mate and mold him into the man you've always wanted" workshops each year, women are left with little more than orange faux tan residue and one-way conversations with the millions of rescue cats adopted each year from local animal shelters they've subsequently renamed "Ewan McGregor" or "David Bowie."

One answer to the lack of even short-term romantic fulfillment is to engage in a practice that men have enjoyed for thousands of years: sex tourism.

Now, I know what you're thinking, Editor: most women found anywhere within the spectrum of this specific life-style demographic are working subpar jobs and could never justify or even afford the expense of two weeks in a five-star resort, let alone the added fees of hiring local male sex workers. Most of these women can't even convince employers to give them adequate time off of work.

Editor, I know. In my article, I will reveal the secrets of finding love during international travel while simultaneously avoiding the high fees that often accompany mainstream, male-centered sex tourism packages.

The first thing women should know is that one need not attempt channeling Elizabeth Gilbert and set standards so high as to snag a polite and willing man with the sweet sexual nectar of Javier Bardem. More often than not, these high expectations are met with an esteem-shattering disappointment too massive to fit in the overhead carry-on department of even the largest international jetliner. Nor shall women set sights on exotic destinations like French Polynesia or Zanzibar.

Standards should be set incredibly low, which should be fairly simple considering some women are so lonely that they have convinced themselves that they are in complicated, long- distance relationships with the men in their volunteer prison literacy programs. Destinations like Cancun or even Tijuana not only offer low-cost travel, but also provide many eager and willing potential matches without the inconvenience of pesky ankle bracelets or other types of government-enforced restraints. These destinations offer surprising opportunities to fulfill unmet needs.

One avenue for a successful sex tourism experience is to abide by some variation of the following itinerary:

First, a woman should end up alone, on a whim in Playa del Carmen, Mexico, en route to an illegal Cuban vacation. This woman should seek out a cheap room as close to the beach as possible, preferably her own private cabana tucked behind a small restaurant that works on some sort of naïve honor system when it comes to self-serve alcohol and fresh tortillas.

Next, this solo female traveler should begin drinking immediately and spend some time sunning her pale, mid-winter flesh in the blistering Caribbean sun. This is the first and most crucial step to prepping for an encounter with a special someone. Dr. Dean Edell reported last month that researchers have scientifically proven that three Coronas with lime and two shots of tequila, followed by two hours face down and asleep in foreign sand fight Seasonal Affective Disorder by 80% and make women 65% more alluring to male travelers (and contribute to male travelers' sex appeal by varying levels), increasing opportunities for love and vacation sex by around 143%.

After the beach face-plant, the solo female traveler should shower, change into another swim suit, throw on a sun dress of questionable length, slide on some flip flops and apply her bottled pheromones, (available for $14.99 through most pleasure party representatives) to the nape of her neck, ensuring her canister of designer pepper spray is tucked safely in her wallet. While her hair is still wet and the third degree sunburn continues to set in–leaving her with an air of sun-kissed, vibrantly glowing sexual mystique–she should peruse the local bars in search of fifty-year-old Canadian tourists to buy her several shots of tequila, peach schnapps and Irish car bombs. She must avoid any large meals in order to reap the full benefits of the free alcohol, while at the same time pacing herself as she eyes the crowd for available bachelors.

Often, touristy destinations like the Mayan Riviera often draw honeymooning couples and corporate conservative types, with the majority employed by large international accounting firms. According to my research, the more conservative men tend to take a liking to women with free spirits, foul mouths, tattoos and radical, leftist politics. I'd advise women to not dismiss these men. Often, they have experienced some degree of internalized oppression and their inner, more sensitive sides can come out of their rough, six-pack-abs exteriors with the right women. And the right amount of alcohol.

After selecting the top choice from what the Playa del Carmen bar scene has to offer, the next step is simple. The solo female traveler should strike up a conversation, and ask if he'd like to take her on a date. 90% of the time, he'll say, "yes." Unlike at domestic single's events, women do not need to impress their newly acquired "friends" with high levels of intelligence, impeccable taste in literature or overly hygienic grooming practices. Men on vacation in Playa del Carmen seldom care about such trivial matters. After the date is an agreed upon next step, the woman and her date should drink more. A lot more. She should visit a fancy restaurant that she is too drunk to sit still in, taking the three-course meal in to-go boxes for consumption at a later time. Then, as a ploy to sober up, she should suggest a quick plunge in the sea.

After a mildly sobering ocean frolic, she should lead her date back to the beach and search for large, black, water-proof mattress-looking props in which to receive a couple's Mexican Milk Massage or Masaje Atractivo de la Leche as it is called in the Riviera. This unique bonding experience is not a regularly advertised service on the beaches of Playa del Carmen so one must saunter (now holding hands with the new fiancé) from one outdoor bar to the next, asking for pints of milk to soothe the sunburn on the back of her crimson thighs. I cannot stress the importance of this step enough. While the sensation of several pints of milk flowing across one's hot, blistering flesh is a surprisingly sexy and albeit healing experience, this ultimate frosty dairy binge sets up an opportunity for another intimate bonding experience later in the evening, when she solicits assistance in cleaning the milk, salt water and sand mix off with the tepid water in her cabana's tiny romantic shower stall. It's like a private high-end spa treatment; only it doesn't cost a cent. And there is the slight possibility of vomiting without him ever noticing.

I will reveal the following steps to "Sex Tourism on a Budget" in the article I wish to write for your magazine.

Editor, this DIY guide is just one example of options women have to take life into their own hands, grasp it like a cheap bottle of Cuervo Gold and drag it into a tangle of unbridled, dizzying holiday passion. Again, I would love an opportunity to share more factual, well-researched scientific information and statistics with your subscribers and can also share advice or stories such as "Ten Steps to Your Very Own Personal Dirty Pretty Woman Weekend in London" as well as "International Grassroots Work in Kenya: An Untapped Resource for Finding a Soulmate."

Again, I thank you for considering my pitch for possible publication in your reputable travel magazine. I look forward to hearing back from you soon.

Your loyal reader, Dani Burlison

Eminem Sex Dreams Decoded

In the thick of the *8 Mile* era, he appears out of nowhere, rescuing me from a pretentious hipster bar. Lanky twenty-somethings sipping two dollar PBRs in their nicotine-soaked white belt adorned skinny jeans avoid eye contact while slouching over bar stools. The room is a thick dark cloud of off-putting pheromones and swollen egos. I grow increasingly restless. A friend excuses herself, stumbling outside with a shaggy-haired bass player and he approaches, politely asking to sit down.

"My name is..." he mumbles, while the indie rock band whines from the stage.

"I know your name," I say, welcoming the attention. "Sit down."

We discuss politics, genetic engineering and needle exchange programs. He invites me to a private screening of a factory farming documentary back at his San Francisco hotel room. Tugging at his baggy trousers, he leads me out of the bar.

Back at the hotel, his passionate rant about dismantling the racist prison industrial complex lures me, without hesitation, into the hotel bed, which is stacked with handmade quilts. "I made those myself," he says.

Eminem is a closet quilter. I am so putting out.

He's just aggressive enough to keep me pleased without hurting me in ways that I don't want to be hurt. His hands are smooth and strong, save for the calluses where the mic is usually firmly grasped. But on this night, my night of an unbridled sexcapade, tangled up in Eminem's hand-sewn rag quilts, the only thing in his hand is my body. Every single naughty bit of it.

As the sun rises, he serves the best organic orange juice ever and asks if I can stay another night. "I have season four of *Sex and the City*," he says, brushing the hair from my eyes. "I love it when Samantha explores her sexuality with that amazing Brazilian artist, Maria. Love should see no boundaries. Let's hold each other and watch it."

He rubs my feet with Ayurvedic sesame oil, leading his hands to all sorts of glorious places on my ravaged body. He makes sweet tender love to me–with the expected intermittent Eminem-style stamina and welcomed throw down–over and over and over again. And again.

I leave the following morning to meet a friend for breakfast. As I dash nutmeg atop my steamed chai, I notice that he, Eminem, is standing in the corner of the cafe, smiling. "I miss you already," he mouths from across the room.

I approach him. He hands over poetry and sketches of boats and hearts he's scrawled across his napkins. "These are for you. I'll never forget you." He looks down, pulls up his drawers and walks away.

I know, Eminem. It feels so empty without me.

He shows up again, repeatedly, over the next ten years. He's always a gentleman, always an animal–sometimes a kitten, sometimes a tiger–in the sack. We meet at airports, on road trips, at campgrounds, in waiting rooms at the veterinarian office. And once in the parking lot at Whole Foods where he carried so many bottles of so much fresh juice. Ten years of the best sex of my life. With Eminem. While I am asleep. Why not Leonard Cohen or Margaret Cho or Mark Wahlberg's character in *I Heart Huckabees?* Eminem is so upset. And isn't it wrong for a feminist to really, really enjoy sex dreams with some dude who, well, hates everyone, everywhere except his kids and Dr. Dre?

What does it all mean?

After shying away from asking my Certified Dream Analyst for insight, I did some research on my own. Here's what some of the experts say:

Freud: If the dream had a ton of penis action already, then maybe Eminem has a pipe in his pants and I need that game piece to play Clue. But that's a different type of pipe. Maybe

I should still look in his pants. Also, the rooms where we always have sex symbolize wombs. I should probably ask my mom but maybe Eminem is my brother. If he is, Freud would still want me to have sex with him, I think.

Jung: It's quite obvious that Slim Shady personifies the shadow archetype. Maybe that's why I keep having sex with him in dark, shadowy places. Is he my animus? Do I want to have more sex with myself? Maybe Eminem's shadow side is vegan and shops at Whole Foods. Maybe I just need a glass of fresh juice.

Laura Ingalls Wilder: I have a lot in common with Eminem. And if good friends are hard to find, maybe Eminem and I should enjoy life on a prairie somewhere. All of our kids would love it.

Radical activist view: Internalized sexism. I hate myself and my girly bits. Maybe I don't care as much about the world as everyone thinks. Maybe deep down I hate women as much as he seems to. Shit. I need to take back the night and challenge oppression. In bed with Eminem. And then cancel my subscription to Ms.

My therapist: What do you think it means?

Power animal: Maybe Eminem is my power animal. I'm not sure what Eminem's native elders think his power animal is, but since he was born in the Year of the Rat, I say it's a rat. The rat is the first animal in Chinese astrology. Maybe Eminem is like an angry Adam and I am his sex-crazed Eve and together we can rule the world. Kind of like Wonder Twins. Or maybe it isn't a rat but a rabbit. Rabbits indicate lots of sex, which leads me back to Freud, and me needing to have sex with Eminem, who might be my brother.

Runes (translated to Norwegian): I thought about my dreams and threw some stones. They read: Marshall elsker du og han ønsker å holde deg varm med hans rage. It's cold in Norway.

Christian view: He needs to be saved. Maybe my life purpose is to smolder Marshall's seething anger with a big, fierce, naked hug. Maybe I need to find God and if I do, maybe he'll lead me to a San Francisco hotel room where I can drink juice. I'm really thirsty.

Annie Lennox: Sweet dreams are indeed, made of these. Maybe Eminem and I want to use and abuse each other. I think we can heal each other. It might be really good for us. Really.

Male friends: You need to stop dating crazy angry guys. You're gonna end up in a trunk.

Female friends: You date wimps. You need to hit that shit. I bet he's actually a really nice guy.

Yoda: If the dark side clouds everything then maybe Eminem's dark public persona just casts a shadow over his sensitive, spiritual side. Maybe I should take him to yoga. And then go out for juice. And watch Star Wars.

Joseph Campbell: If dreamtime leads us to permanent fixtures in our psyches then maybe Eminem is a part of me, like a twin, and contrary to Freud's wishes, we shouldn't have sex because that would be incest or something and I'm pretty sure incest is illegal, especially for twins. Also, Campbell says dreams support our conscious lives so maybe Eminem is my sugar daddy and I should just ask him to support me and buy me the house he offered up in my 6th dream about him.

Oprah: If living my best life means that it doesn't get better than sex dreams about Eminem than maybe I should leave it at that and not have sex with him. Maybe I'd end up on fire. Or in his trunk. With no juice. I wouldn't like that.

Confucius: "What the superior man seeks is in himself; what the small man seeks is in others." Maybe Eminem lost something in that first dream and he keeps coming back for sex because he's trying to find it in my pants. Maybe I need an X-ray so I can find it for him and send it in the mail so the dreams stop.

Wizardry and other assorted magic. Namely, the wisdom of Albus Dumbledore: If it does not do to dwell on dreams and forget to live, then I think that maybe Dumbledore thinks the only way to make sense of the dreams is to live this all out, either through sex with Eminem or with a stand-in or body double or what have you. Dumbledore also says that happiness can be found in the darkest of times, if one only remembers to turn on the light. Slim Shady needs to come to the light, I think. And I think the light is in my pants and in his pants, too. But what does Dumbledore know? He got smoked by Snape. Maybe he don't know shit.

Eminem: I think he's reaching out to me, telepathically, and that maybe he'd see this as an opportunity to seize everything he ever wanted and have sex with me. And that I am his portal to show the world that he's socially conscious and is a really gifted quilter and he needs me to help him set up some quilting classes through an adult education program. Or maybe I'm just more thirsty than I realize and I do, in fact, need some juice.

Stop Making Sense

"When a man does something that offends us, there is probably a good reason for it," beamed the well-dressed and attractive 30-something from the stage. "Men are simply responding to us and we need to give them the benefit of the doubt. Learn how to communicate in a way that men understand and you'll get the results you want." The audience smiled, nodded and continued to stare with wide eyes and unwavering attention toward the stage. I was baffled.

One lone and uncomfortable soul among a sea of eager and desperate women, I sat patiently in the comfort of an air-conditioned San Francisco hotel conference room hoping to learn the secrets of men–longing for the fading light bulb in my head to magically spark on and illuminate my mind. Curious and confused, yet still quite often impressed by the various men in my life, a friend pointed me in the direction of PAX Programs and the array of workshops they offer to teach women how to obtain, maintain and appreciate relationships with men. My friend assured me that the programs are worth the pricey $450 weekend workshops and that her life and relationships with men have been forever altered as a result of attendance. I felt optimistic and headed to a free three-hour introductory night in hopes of catching the "Making Sense of Men" fever that had fired up countless women before me.

The speaker carried on, explaining how women have unrealistic expectations of men, how women tend to take everything personally and how women who are not receptive to men and their offers of gifts–and basic assistance like opening doors–cause men to leave relationships or avoid them altogether. The divorced 40-something next to me shot me a slightly perplexed glance that I reflected back at her without the slightest hesitation. Still exuding enthusiastic confidence, the presenter went on to share that men cannot multitask, can only listen at certain times of the day, become uninterested when our self-confidence falters and that women are the multitasking Velcro of the universe. I took a deep breath and patiently waited to hear the revolutionary information that I was promised.

PAX Programs began in the early 1990s as a response to one woman's quest to understand members of the male gender and to have happy, healthy relationships with them. After a divorce in her mid-20s, PAX founder Alison Armstrong threw herself into the study of all things men: how they think, how they feel, what they want. Though Armstrong does not hold a degree in sociology, anthropology or any of the behavioral sciences, and has no formal training in scientific research methods, she spent several years in dialogue with the men in her life in order to gain perspective. As she began noticing patterns of thought and behavior in the men she interviewed, she felt that this information could benefit countless other women and decided to share her findings at small, casual, women-only gatherings. The small groups were well received and eventually led to larger seminars that now consist of half- a-dozen workshops including "Celebrating Men, Satisfying Women," "Celebrating Men and Marriage" and even one or two on empowering women. All workshops are taught by women for all-female audiences and satisfaction is guaranteed or participants get a full refund.

The seminars promise to provide women with the tools and terminology that PAX says are essential in order to maintain satisfying relationships with not only male mates, but our fathers, brothers, co-workers and sons, as well. Some past attendees claim that the workshops have even changed interactions with random men in places like grocery stores and banks. Graduates of PAX Programs insist that they now live new and fulfilling lives, gracefully coasting through the world with newfound vocabularies, attitudes and confidence as women. They all swear that they now get exactly what they want from men and find that they are less frustrated and upset by the various male/female interactions they previously experienced.

At the core of PAX teachings is the message that women need to change language and behavior in order to get men to just take out the damn trash–because, as I learned in the intro night, men are providers, not *doers,* and they need to be asked to do things (in a very specific way, I might add).

Men can't take the initiative unless there is something in it for them. It is also heavily implied that men are set in their ways and are unable and not expected to evolve in the same ways that women have. With this information women should have the ability to see men in a different light and will therefore stop expecting too much. Again, men are apparently only responding to our behavior. If we act "right," men will conduct themselves accordingly.

One benefit of PAX Programs is the communication style that is taught. Like any non-confrontational, emotion-owning language, it can be utilized for dialogue between anyone at any time, regardless of gender. PAX teaches exactly what parents learn in "positive discipline" classes when the kiddos are acting out, wreaking havoc on our homes and attacking preschool mates with magic markers or jars of bugs: no passive-aggressive criticism or nagging and heavy on the positive reinforcement. Furthermore, anyone who has so much as watched a movie with a couple's therapy scene can understand and recognize the typical "I" statements that are meant to be non-confrontational: "I feel hurt when I feel ignored"...or, better, "I feel super-annoyed when you are watching fricken anime on your laptop while I clean, mediate the kids' latest conflict, make dinner and get ready for the party that we're already late for." PAX takes these models of effective communication, throws in a twist of subtle biological determinism (think: manifest destiny, only between men and women) and voila! Positive female-to-male interaction!

What makes PAX unique is that the workshop presenters do their best to highlight differences between how they believe men and women think, feel and communicate, focusing on the behaviors that they suggest men have inherited and passed down over time–since the caveman days, they say. Examples include the inability to multitask (they *really* drive this one home) and the overwhelming desire to have sex with women who are blessed with long, shiny hair and shapely bodies. As much as it is pointed out that men have not evolved, it is of equal importance, according to PAX, to understand that women have. Women may need to *revolve* and make lifestyle adjustments to accommodate those differences. PAX also emphasizes the need for women to help restore men's power and strongly suggests that women stop alienating men, and do so by learning "Menglish." By speaking a language that men can truly understand and will quickly and wholeheartedly respond to, ladies can avoid common miscommunication problems that result in hurt feelings and subsequent breakups. Women, say PAX workshop facilitators, tend to make assumptions about the information they receive from men. When men mention possibilities of future dates, trips, etc., women hear promises that often go unfulfilled. And that, quite frankly, just pisses us off and leads to a heap of hurt feelings on both ends.

PAX Programs spokeswoman Patrice McKinley asserts that the workshops promote peaceful partnerships based on mutual understanding and mutual appreciation. "The information we provide gives women and men a different way of relating to one another that brings out the best in both of them," she writes in an email to the *Pacific Sun*. "A simple, yet powerful shift in the point of view of the opposite sex can result in pure ecstasy and satisfaction."

Maybe I have overindulged myself with the writings of people like bell hooks and Angela Davis, but I am fairly attached to the pride I carry as a woman, knowing that my foremothers worked their asses off for me to be recognized as a human being who is equal to men. I also have a great number of men in my life who do indeed multitask and work consciously and diligently to challenge patriarchy by engaging in the tough and humbling work to acknowledge–and correct–their privileged roles in our sexist society. Honestly, these experiences factor heavily into my personal inability to jump onto the PAX train and just chug along with the masses. Still, I wanted to learn more about the PAX philosophy and why it wouldn't sink in for me.

I dove deeper. I spoke with women who had participated in the workshops, and they either loved the workshops–or hated them. I borrowed a colleague's seminar notes, read Alison Armstrong's articles and even listened to a PAX CD during a weekend road trip with friends. Still, as a strong feminist woman in the trenches single-handedly raising two daughters, I was flabbergasted and offended. My mind repeatedly referenced the infamous, and possibly apocryphal, 1955 "Good Wife's Guide" in *Housekeeping Monthly,* in which the woman's role as a secondary and less important participant in the relationship is clearly detailed. Also, I was sick of hearing about oxytocin and how it supposedly justified human behavior.

I still had more questions. What about those of us who naturally or consciously defy traditional gender stereotypes with the hope that someday our kids will feel confident in expressing themselves, knowing that both women *and* men strive to understand one another? What about transgender men and women? What about bisexual men and women? What about men and women with distinct cultural differences? And what about drag queens? Although PAX has recently begun offering a new workshop titled "Celebrating Black Men, Satisfying Black Women," it doesn't appear that the myriad diverse lifestyles and backgrounds are taken into account and that PAX instead makes sweeping generalizations, which reinforce the traditional gender roles that simply don't work for everyone in today's changing and fun (drag queens!) times. Maybe it's simple and the demographic of men that Alison Armstrong interviewed while doing her research live on a different planet from my male friends.

I would like to believe that all humans have evolved from the ideologies of the Dark Ages (aside from a handful of extremely backward sexists and white supremacist wing nuts). I've read of amazing humans of both genders setting world records, building rocket ships that blast through space and even removing foreign matter from inside of *brains–all* of which we would never have dreamed of witnessing as a species even just 100 short years ago. Women and men have created musical and artistic masterpieces and have saved entire generations with the invention of medications and conflict- resolving communication techniques. It is for these reasons and because of the amazing, multitasking men in my life that I have faith that men have the ability to take out the trash and communicate openly–at the same time, even! Reinforcing gender stereotypes does little more than disempower women and encourage men to carry on as barbaric, simple-minded doofuses.

As the program concluded, I was no longer perplexed, but felt anxious and annoyed as I gathered my things, passed the table of products that would presumably change my life and headed outside. Knowing that I couldn't justify forking over a chunk of my rent money for a weekend workshop that would teach me the mysterious "six words" women should use in order to get men to do what they want–and come back offering to do more!–I was also a little bitter. "So that's it?" I asked myself. "If I don't go to the workshops and join this PAX movement then am I just screwed and deserve the miscommunication that comes up in my relationships?"

As I pondered the question while pushing my way out onto the hot San Francisco street, I also understood how the programs have become so successful. People, regardless of gender, are looking for answers to all sorts of tough questions. Generally, we tend to feel more open to receiving them in well-structured formats like 12-step meetings, churches or organizations like Landmark forums. People also feel more secure when the information they are seeking comes from authority figures. Alison Armstrong is a marketing genius and her presenters are strong, confident women who provide fun, engaging conversations that are easily absorbed if one is curious and desperate enough to make changes in relationships with men. Still, some of us feel the forum only lets men and their choices off the hook, leaving the burden of relationship work on women and our pocketbooks.

I held the door open for the 40-something divorcee and she looked at me, astonishment blazing from her face.

"Did they just spend three hours telling us that it's all our fault and all our responsibility?" she asked, flustered at the thought of returning to the dating world after the end of a 20-year marriage.

We walked in silence for a few moments, but were thinking the exact same thing:

"Yup. They totally did."

DIY Ecstatic Dance Jam

1. The first step to planning your very own personal Ecstatic Dance Jam is to thoroughly reflect on whether or not an Ecstatic Dance Jam is the right thing for you. You may want to find a quiet place to sit and ask yourself questions like...

- Do I enjoy documentaries about Whirling Dervishes but wish they were slightly unkempt, spinning with their shirts off, moonstone necklaces glistening against their hairy chests?

- Do I love warm, dimly lit and poorly ventilated rooms?

- Do I enjoy being in close proximity with sweaty men and women who do not believe in antiperspirant, who instead feel that bodies will "self clean" if just left alone?

- Do I really believe that dance is sacred and that it can, like, really take me on a journey?

- Do I enjoy unconventional cardio workouts?

- Do I become giddy at the mere mention of "embodied play," "soul activation," or "vibrational sound healing"?

- If you answered yes to any of these questions, you may be ready to ecstatically jam on the dance floor.

2. The next step to creating an Ecstatic Dance Jam is to find attendees that share the same feelings about sweat, drumming, raw foods and saffron-dyed fabric. Again, find a quiet place, practice deep breathing and tap into your intuition's core. It will lead you to the people you need to invite. If you live near power lines or a cell phone tower and find that their unnatural energy or radioactive waves create a barrier between you and your clairvoyance (and you loaned your tin foil hat to your aunt Freya), there are other avenues to finding the group of Ecstatic Dance Jammers that will mesh well with you in your sacred space. Places to seek these jamming dancers include the Whole Foods raw desert aisle and Earth Day festivals. You may also spot potential guests dancing to jam bands at the local farmers market or pedaling pot brownies or other cannabis-rich snacky treats at reggae concerts. And of course, don't forget the 7 a.m. naked yoga class at the nearest hot spring resort. Also, tantra workshops, crop circle study groups and your neighborhood psychic institute are well worth looking into for attendees. Tip: Men wearing linen pants and no underwear are always game for Ecstatic Dance.

3. Make a shopping list. You will need very specific edibles at your Ecstatic Dance Jam. Acai juice, raw cacao, vegan, and gluten-free raw nut paste for slathering onto organic vegetables sticks are all hot items. You'll also need electromagnetic charged water, kombucha, mate, various tinctures, magical elixirs and fresh coconut juice, straight from the nut (which double as hats, bowls or breast shields, reducing your carbon foot print. Bingo!). It might be a good idea to also stock up on massage oils, animal friendly personal lubricant, hypoallergenic condoms, mouthwash and tea tree oil hand sanitizer. You can never be too prepared for the needs that may arise at an Ecstatic Dance Jam.

4. Probably the most important step to setting up your own Ecstatic Dance Jam is to prepare your body and spirit. In order to brush up on Ecstatic Dance Jam moves, rent as many DVDs as possible on Pentecostal Snake Handling, Zumba, various tribal dance practices and most importantly, recorded exorcisms. Slink into a favorite leotard and warm up by jumping, waving your arms and spinning in circles–all at the same time (be sure to remove glassware, ceramic Goddess sculpture and other items from your practice space before hand. Training for Ecstatic Dance Jams can break a lot of valuable shit). If you don't have access to electronics like a television set or DVD player, an alternate approach to preparing your body for the night of boundary-less, sweaty grooving and flailing is to think back to a time when you or someone you love had food poisoning. Remember the violent heaving? Reenact that. While standing up. Or visualize a swarm of angry bees or Jehovah's Witnesses approaching you early on a bright crisp Saturday morning. Go into full-on five pointed star pose and then begin swinging your arms wildly, as if swatting said bees and Jehovah's Witnesses away with the aggression of divine, otherworldly energy. That is good practice, too.

5. Finally, it's time to start thinking about ambiance for the

Ecstatic Dance Jam. Smudge your Ecstatic Dance Jam Space with sage, smoldering Palo Santo wood, patchouli oil, what have you. Adding floral scented incense into the mix–like rose or jasmine–is always a nice touch. It won't diminish the overwhelming presence of body odor in the room, but will make it more difficult for attendees to pinpoint which body exudes the most intensely sour aroma. You'll also need props like sitars, bongo drums, lots and lots of silk scarfs, maybe a tambourine or two. You're probably thinking to yourself, "What about candles?" Candles actually create a huge fire hazard with all of those exposed locks of body hair, flowing fabric and belly chains flying around in a cramped space like your garage. Its better to include those only in your restroom or another "chill" environment you create for your guests. After the space is mostly set up, an altar with figurines vaguely resembling genitals is essential to rounding out your ecstasy-inducing space. Tip: Don't forget collections of Rumi poetry. Ecstatic Dance Jammers eat that shit up.

6. When guest begin to arrive, remember this is a safe place to express yourself without fear or judgment. Every dance move is acceptable at an Ecstatic Dance Jam. Remember that kid who threw himself across the floor of the bank last Friday? The drunk girl chasing her boyfriend out of the taqueria with shoes in hand the day before that? The mime in front of the coffee shop downtown, acting out a scene from Houdini untying himself inside an underwater coffin? All of these moves are welcome. Invited. Cherished. Take off, fly, sweat. It's Ecstatic Dance Jam time.

Part 2:

Other Kinds of Things

The Geography Of Uncool:
Public Transportation

When my last relationship succumbed to a burning mass of repulsively toxic, gaseous flames at the same time that my pathetic little Volvo chugged up its last puny hill, the idea of starting fresh in a new environment was appealing. Instead of dumping money into car repairs or crying over some jerkwad, I'd embark on an adventure, using the bus for my forty-mile commute. My plan was to appreciate the newfound freedom from my horrible boyfriend and unreliable car while catching up on some reading aboard the bus. If at some point I crossed paths with a fellow wayward commuter, great. A little innocent on-board flirtation would be a welcome bonus at the start of my new life.

At the time, public transportation cradled the promise of

possibility; romance, adventure and a microscopic carbon footprint. A winning situation for me and the entire world.

To psych myself up, I thought back to several years ago when I watched Amelie every single night for an entire month in an attempt to revive my faith in love. I figured that if I watched the film often and with the naïvely optimistic, rose-tinted eyes of someone far enough away from the obliteration of heartbreak, that I'd somehow manifest some osmotic boot- knocking. Or something like that. Of course, what made the movie a complete romantic masterpiece wasn't solely the onscreen presence of the lovely miss Audrey Tautou or hottie Mathieu Kassovitz and their much-anticipated kiss on her doorstep, but the element of mystery, adventure and hip-quotient that Paris' public transportation system and its depots seem to exude.

The idea of a chance encounter with a potential mate in the middle of criss-crossing strangers at a bus or train station or while daydreaming out the window, rolling swiftly toward a destination is one that I'd argue most of us have entertained at least once in our lifetimes.

My version would go something like this: Girl drops polyurethane-free water bottle or Patti Smith memoir. Boy reaches under seat to retrieve it for her. They brush hands. Soon, they are brushing naughty bits in a dimly lit Paris hotel room. Who hasn't fantasized about this? And regardless of the sex we may or may not be having after traveling en masse with a pack of strangers, going from one place to the next is an adventure. And who on God's green earth doesn't love adventure?

Unfortunately, Paris lies far from my humble abode and my

community has yet to provide folks like me with a wonderful travel rail. I have no L Train. I have no Jeff Tweedy kissing and swaying on the CTA. I have no BART. Instead, I have a once-an-hour bus system where stations resemble anything but Paris in the springtime. Gare du Nord is an architectural delight and a glorious god damn carnival of love. Most Golden Gate Transit stations are not.

Still, the experience was pleasant enough at first. And I felt righteous about the fact that my Volvo was no longer polluting the Northern California ecosystem. The first few weeks brought with them a handful of bright young backpackers with sun kissed cheeks and the fragrance of adventure seeping from their pores heading to and from San Francisco. The mean bus driver that always yelled at everyone barely fazed me as I lived vicariously through the travelers' stories, nostalgia for my own travel experiences aboard foreign buses carrying through my days.

However, after a few short weeks of commuting, I learned rather quickly that there are few things as unappealing, uncool and unromantic as navigating the suburban public transportation system.

Eventually, summer gave way to fall, and the tourists bailed, leaving me alone with the grumbly old bus driver, at least two highly intoxicated insurance agents, a handful of transients with upper respiratory infections–who repeatedly failed to shield their warm, moist coughs near the narrow aisle–and at least twenty others with no sense of personal boundaries on each trip.

My fantasies of love were replaced with the reality of the public-transportation-utilizing demographic of where I live. My open heart closed like a cold hard bear trap on the paws of hope. Daily, I found myself restraining my inner crazy bus lady rants: If I am riding the bus that means I am broke and don't have a car! That doesn't mean that I am desperately horny and looking to replace my last douchebag boyfriend with another! The fact that I am on a bus is also not an open invitation to continuously bounce, brush or stroke your leg up against mine! Stop fucking touching me!

Bus travel provides its own mobile and unsanitary culture. Vomiting or urinating on the bus occurs more frequently than one would expect. People smuggle live critters like small, tropically colored birds and Siamese cats past the driver almost daily. An astounding number of passengers–usually men between twenty-five and thirty-seven, roughly–have awful taste in music, blasting Linkin Park from their headphones. Younger men blare auto-tunes, likely recorded at home on their iPhones. And high school girls ditching algebra–the most loathed passengers of all–screech and shit-talk in close proximity when all I want to do is melt into my novel, slather on hand sanitizer and weep.

Yet the constant exposure to inappropriate behavior allowed me some room to lower my own self-imposed standards of socially acceptable behavior as well. First, I basically started hating everyone around me. I was the mean bitch than no one wanted to sit near anymore. I didn't offer thanks when drunk men gulping forty-ouncers complimented my eyes at eight o'clock in the morning. I stopped pretending to listen when re- entry students attempted to engage me in discussions about their economics midterms. And instead of judging, I began condoning the mothers who yelled at their bratty children. Those little fuckers deserved it. I even felt that it was perfectly fine to deliver my stool sample to the lab via bus, though it did make me wonder just how many people ride the bus with stool samples tumbling around inside their satchels. And if not stool samples, what other public transit health code violations are tucked away in the various backpacks strewn about?

The bus was turning me into an awful person. Amelie would never behave like this.

The anxious moodiness didn't last long before it was replaced with the overwhelming presence of a deep dark depression and humiliating sense of defeat. Like a detrimental relapse from substance abuse recovery or a gambling addiction, I started lying to loved ones about where I was spending my time and how I was getting from one place to the next. I refused to acknowledge that I was not a glamorous writer, living a glamorous life with book signings and glamorous suitors lined up outside my door. I was ashamed that I began singling out my best dating options at bus stops–usually homeless thirty-somethings with skateboards and scruffy beards–and wondered if they were my only options, being that I now traveled by bus right alongside them.

And with my motion sickness, I was smacked with the esteem- shattering realization that at any moment I could be someone else's horror story, vomiting into my lunch bag. Or worse.

Finally, I made my way to the doctor's office, hoping I'd return home with a new prescription for anti-depressants. I engaged in daily battles between walking aboard or throwing myself under the buses that constantly rolled past. I needed something to take the edge off.

"I'm not sure if my health issues are causing my depression but I feel awful," I whined. "The whole bus ride here, I just wanted to die."

"Oh, you're riding the bus?" she asked. "Tell me more about that."

Poor me. I ranted on and on, explaining the time it takes to get to work, to get my youngest daughter to school and how hard it is to transport groceries by bike. I explained how the bus driver made me cry after scolding me for using too much change, how bros with leg tattoos always sit next to me on their way to DUI school, pretending to sleep in order to let their hands rest gently against my thighs and how the other day, while waiting for my bus, I saw an elderly man with no teeth trying to eat an apple. An apple. With no teeth. Times don't get much harder than that.

"I don't think you need antidepressants, Dani," She said, alarm spreading across her face. "You need to stop riding the bus."

And she's right. Public transportation is ruining my life.

In the end, I know my lazy ass should be grateful that I am even allowed to ride the bus with my horrible, shitty attitude. But Amelie, no matter how sweet and hygienic, would never willingly surround herself with dirty-handed people who regularly wet their pants and try to grope thirty-something women just trying to read their damn books.

My dreams have been shattered.

My friends say I should be more open minded and not dismiss the possibility of finding love in an unexpected place and that my unfaltering sense of humor is a testament that I am still relatively cool, regardless of my daily bus trips. While I like to think this is true, I doubt my soulmate is anything like the fifty-year-old **Hanna Barbera** enthusiast who rubbed himself excitedly behind me while discussing Smurfette and Wilma Flintstone a few weeks ago. Or maybe he is. Who am I to judge? I ride the bus, after all.

Hired Help

Quite a bit is revealed about someone's character when visiting their home. Squeaky-clean kitchen counters and alphabetized cookbook shelves usually mean the home's inhabitants are well organized and function best with structure. Stacks of reference books towering next to sofas and back issues of the *New Yorker* strewn across coffee tables usually indicate that the residents are excellent conversationalists. Little Zen sand trays in entryways, prayer flags across doorways and Yogi Tea bag quotes designed in nifty mandala patterns under refrigerator magnets may mean the residents have spiritual leanings, although everyone knows that people with too much clutter can't *really* like Thich Nat Hahn or the Dalai Lama that much. Broken windows, doors struggling to stay attached to hinges and faulty (or entirely absent) plumbing mechanisms mean the people dwelling in these types of homes are either complete psychopaths or have very lazy landlords. Porno mags left on the back of the toilet usually mean it's a good time to bust out the disposable toilet seat covers tucked in your purse.

The only thing that reveals more about a person than simply dropping by their apartment for a quick martini after a Thursday night Zumba class, is working for them. As a housekeeper.

Housekeepers have up-close-and-personal access to people and their varied and bizarre habits. We catch glimpses of– and sometimes become frighteningly aware of–very intimate details about people. Many are often oblivious of this despite the fact that we are often washing their 8-gazillion count Egyptian cotton sheets and disposing of all of the interesting things they toss into the trash and recycling bins. We mop up their messes. We make their kids' beds and organize their bookshelves.

I say "we" even though it is embarrassing to admit–I am one woman in the vast and growing population of housekeepers. I have, and sometimes still do, clean other people's homes for extra cash.

People often think little to nothing of the hired help that clean their homes, rarely entertaining thoughts of how this type of work stood out as an employment option for so many. We all know that no child in the history of the world ever stood up and proudly declared, "I want to be a maid when I grow up, Mommy!" It has never happened. I can guarantee it. Still, many of us find ourselves face down in mop buckets, sloshing across floors that we see no more than once or twice a week.

For me, it wasn't my dabbling into the world of Eastern spirituality and its non-attachment and Seva (selfless service) philosophies that led me into the world of tossing strangers' silk panties into the delicate cycle. Nor was it a curiosity of how the other half (the half that can afford housecleaners) lived. It was sheer desperation. The threat of ending up homeless again. The fear of never having enough to feed my children. Cleaning the homes of strangers always put cash in my pocket, even if that cash only amounted to an extra fifty bucks a week. Fifty bucks meant gas in my shitty car. Fifty bucks meant my kids could have snacks between meals or could attend a handful of some kind of academically, culturally or spiritually enriching after school activities. When money wasn't so tight, fifty bucks also meant that Mama sometimes got a much-needed night out on the town.

I'm aware that I've been more fortunate than others, who spend forty or more hours per week in the esteem-crushing work of housekeeping, bless their souls. It hasn't always been awful, either. But it has always been eye opening.

One thing I've learned about being the hired help is that it is always more comfortable to clean someone's home when the house is empty; while the residents are off shopping, working, having their hair frosted or feathered or whatever the current fad is. My favorite client was rarely home when I arrived to clean. A feminist psychotherapist, she seemed to really feel good about helping my struggling single-mom-grad-student self out. She'd leave kind yellow Post-it notes next to her entertainment center: *Dear Dani, no need to vacuum the upstairs this week. Feel free to listen to this new Santana CD. It rocks!* So I would. I'd slip the disk into the player, imagining the limited release 2003 Chateau St. Something

Sauvignon Blanc she and her husband would knock back later that night, while Santana's sweet guitar licks slipped through her study and into the kitchen. By then, I'd be home counting my bills, hoping that in addition to my salary from my other part-time job, my four cleaning jobs that week would mean I could pay my rent.

On occasion, I brought my own CDs. Nothing like Metallica's Ride the Lightning to get in gear for some serious fucking dust removal in someone else's house. Sometimes, this particular family would hire me for events, like their big Passover Seder. I'd stand at attention in the kitchen, a lone, weary butleress, waiting to clear plates from the table, serve dessert and wash the antique dinnerware one by one, drying each carefully before returning them to their special china cabinet. I'd eavesdrop on the family discussing recent trips to Paris, Istanbul, their apartment in Manhattan, all the while praying that my car would start at the end of the evening so I could drive the twenty miles back home, pay the sitter and start in on my own dishes before finishing term papers and packing up the following day's lunch for my kids.

Sometimes, I'd work as a team with a fellow single mom friend. Meredith and I would scrub the floors of an indoor smoker, a woman with seventeen rescue cats who worked as a Russian translator for the CIA in her home office. She had an extensive collection of tiny fragile figurines. We cleaned them one by one while she coughed and puffed away, shouting over the phone in Russian. We always left reeking of a back alley, chain-smoking dumpster dive in close proximity to a frequent health code violating cat food factory.

We hit the jackpot–or so we thought–when we were hired on as regular cleaning ladies for a local alternative healing clinic. The clinic's owner, a seemingly nice pseudo-hippy with a spiritual connection to her darling opium poppy garden, gave us keys asking only that we tidy the place up sometime on Sundays, when the clinic was closed. The first few months were virtually effortless. We'd let ourselves in after slow- moving mornings of coffee and day-old crois-sants at the local cafe and begin our wiping and scrubbing, pacing ourselves along to the rhythm of whatever New Age melodies we could tolerate from the CD player. The inner environment of the health clinic, even this one owned by an opium growing Rastafarian wannabe, was generally spot-less. I'd take the upstairs restroom and treatment rooms; Meredith would conquer the downstairs kitchen, apoth-ecary and waiting area.

Our time at the clinic came to a screeching halt one cloudy Sunday afternoon when we were met with a bathtub three or more inches full of pubic hair, along with empty enemas tossed across the bathroom floor. The owner's response to our refusal to ever again dispose of what appeared to be a small nation's shaving ritual gone awry? *Sometimes people need to do things to make themselves feel good.*

We wondered if she even considered the number of voodoo dolls we could have needle felted all of that hair into.

We'd polish the Legos of home-schooled kids, vacuum dis-carded weed and broken glass out of closets during move-out cleanings, peel paper plates–crusted together with wet cat food–off of kitchen floors. We'd gag as we ran rotten fish from stovetops to outdoor waste bins and tossed skid-marked tighty-whiteys into washing machines with the help of pliers.

And it made no difference how kind the bosses were, how much cleaning prep the owners did beforehand or how much they paid (note: the going rate at the time, circa 2003-2007, was about $50 a pop), the fact was, I was scraping pricey, molding basque sheep cheese off of the same Heath Ceramics that I wanted, ironing toddler-sized Burberry trousers and dusting rare ivory carvings and all other sorts of things I'm pretty sure I still can't afford, before driving home to eat leftover beans and rice.

Filtering the Kitty-Cat Almond Roca out of fancy litter boxes and shoveling dog poop wasn't very fun, either.

And it wasn't just that it was quite awkward to stumble upon pornography or enema bags. It was how we, the hired help, felt about ourselves when we went out into the world–Bon Ami powder rinsed from our hands, fresh clothes replacing the jeans which molding orange juice gushed onto just hours before. It was almost a secret, a taboo for us–my friend and I–both mothers, spending our kid-free time picking up after the kids of strangers. Throwing out expired yogurt and wilted lettuce. The wastefulness, that crushed me the most.

Still, we, a lot of us, do these things. Sometimes we have to. We set out, applying our skills in any way we can in order to make ends meet. We drop expensive, unworn clothes off at Goodwill for people who can afford not to sell them on eBay for a few extra bucks. We sanitize the toys of strangers' kids while our own are home with babysitters. We slouch, we tweak our necks dusting rafters, we listen to Santana, spill sour fluids down our clothes in a hurry and suck it the hell up to tie together a living for ourselves. We do our best. And unfortunately, doing our best sometimes means we need to dispose of twenty pounds of pubic hair shavings.

Sometimes we throw a fit while pouring expensive wine down a drain, imagining what it tasted like a few days before. And yes, sometimes we are shocked, encountering bondage gear where we least expect it; usually tucked around some dark corner, resting quietly alongside our humility.

Pasty Little Inner Mutt

For the last few years, I have driven past a small, drab community center called Sons of Norway. The building, set off of the street in a questionable part of town, often appears to be empty, unused and possibly even abandoned. On occasion, I've entertained the idea that this Norwegian gathering spot is not the cultural heritage site it claims to be, but rather a front for some sort of white supremacy group or drug-dealing mafia. I mean, who can imagine a bunch of old white men with silly hats doing anything but causing trouble?

Still, as someone fascinated with the idea of Norse role- play involving some of the Gods and Goddesses of my own Scandinavian roots, my inner skeptic became intrigued.

I imagined a variety of magical things happening behind the walls of the lodge, which is named after a Norse goddess. In my best-case daydream, the members host women-positive pagan rituals, drink mead from viking ship-engraved chalices and throw runes to foresee the future. Pelts of Nordic reindeer would cover hand-carved benches crafted from Norwegian spruce and maple. Maybe some of the members were even in Norwegian Black Metal bands and hosted hardcore events, complete with slide shows of burning churches, a la *Until the Light Takes Us.* At the very least, I fully expected lessons on how to hammer out my own functioning bronze helmet and to embroider hand spun wool with the pre-Christian symbols of my roots.

As I have recently committed to further exploring and sharing my own heritage with my children, I decided to do some research on this tiny little building and the people who gather in it. The simple website informed me that the venue holds many events, including traditional Norwegian dance performances and language and art classes for youth. Aside from the gnarly lutefisk dinners, Sons of Norway appeared to be a decent enough organization. The only thing holding me back from immediately signing on as a member was the idea of explaining to my peers why I'd be spending my weekends in a secret clubhouse with hoards of old white men.

Here, in the land of celebrating cultural diversity and cramming tolerance down each other's throats, most Californians assert themselves as almost self-righteously open-minded. So much so, that any membership with a European-affiliated organization could easily deem one a racist. As a result, well-meaning white communities such as my own often denounce their heritage and instead, unknowingly engage in cultural appropriation and gentrification, clinging to the "exotic" in order to either fit in or appear interesting. For a lot of Caucasians, being white or of European descent isn't cool unless you come from a long line of political revolutionaries or gypsies. The only thing more uncool than having white genes is celebrating a fighting, pillaging group of Vikings. It's not politically correct and carries too much baggage, so it's better to ignore it. Or to wear a sari and change your name from "Sarah" to "Shakti."

And although the intentions are misguided, I get it, really. Many white Americans are so far removed from deep connections to ancestral lands or any type of cultural heritage that they feel lost and maybe even a little jealous for what others have in regards to tradition and connection to place. So people watch TV and go to Disneyland and replace their inherited cultural rituals with shopping and then wonder why they feel disconnected. On top of that sense of detachment is the lumping together of people of all different pigment-lacking backgrounds into one big pot of creamy whiteness, regardless of where the family trees sprout from. This can result in a weakened sense of identity. And generally speaking, most white people have ancestral roots associated with oppression of non-white people, whether through active participation in genocide or just plain ignorance. And no one with even the dimmest spark of decency wants to be associated with genocide or oppression.

So, to really, truly embrace ancestral roots, most white Americans would have to dress as if every day is a trip to the Renaissance Fair. And no one wants to look like ***Braveheart*** or a 15th-century peasant girl. Well, some people do, but nobody wants to talk to them except other people who also frequent Renaissance Fairs. Plus the food is bad. Tamales and curries are so much better than mutton or fermented trout. So people deny their roots and adopt the cultural practices of others in attempts to present themselves as open-minded or culturally inclusive. Others–particularly in the region of the world I live in–embark on familial expeditions, digging deep through their heritage to locate even the smallest sliver of non-white lineage in order to prove a point, clinging to their variation in genes to utilize as street cred. And for me, although it is rumored that somewhere along the line a woman of Native American decent took up residency in my own family tree, I remain saturated with a smörgåsbord of the whitest genes this side of Snowflake, the albino gorilla. There is no way aroundit. This, I believe, is something worthy of examining.

With no Daughters of Germany or A Little Bit Historically Oppressed Scots-Irish or I Might Be Native American But I'm Not Really Sure organizations nearby, I decided to risk rumors that my involvement with Sons of Norway would be misconstrued as a descent into a white supremacist society. I set out to meet this small fraction of my people, hoping for a sense of belonging.

The thing I noticed at my first trip is that everyone looked like they belonged at my father's family reunion, sans the mystery casseroles and jello salads. Most attendees were really old and really white, with blue eyes and aesthetically offensive sweaters. The men were enormous, with the giant farming hands of the Midwestern stock they were born into. The room filled with North Dakota accents in lieu of the Swedish Chef voice I had so desperately longed to hear. Everyone sipped instant coffee from styrofoam cups.

There were no murals of Norwegian fjords, no kinetic Viking ship sculptures, no statues of Thor or Leif Ericson, no battle scene reenactments and no one close to my age at this small town Viking Fest. There were no chalices of mjød , or mead, to be found. And there were certainly no Norwegian Black Metal band members strolling the grounds with crazy tattoos. After a brief introduction to handmade ring maille armor construction and a quick lesson on identifying ancient Nordic coins, I looked into rosemåling classes for my kids, ate bread with gjetost–a very brown and very salty goat cheese–and returned a few months later to learn more.

Despite the lack of action in the form of the hollering, bearded Vikings I'd hoped to meet, I am learning a lot about the emigration, food and music of these white folks whose genes I share. Yet, as was my Scandinavian ancestors experienced when first arriving on the barren prairies of the American Midwest, I've been slightly disappointed and still don't quite mesh with this community. And it is quite likely that I may never find a place outside of my home where I'll really fit in. Like most Americans, I am a diluted mix of European blood with a sprinkling of a few other tidbits mixed in along the way. There are few made from the exact same recipe as my siblings and I. Regardless, I am learning to find my place and embracing my pasty little inner mutt.

I'll keep visiting the hall in attempts to uncover some links to my past. And until my fantasy of bronze head wear and fleeting thoughts of forming a flute and bass Nordic Metal Band called Valhöller with my friend come to fruition, my daughter's hand-crafted aluminum foil Viking helmet and my OE Synth Norsk/Darkthrone Pandora station will have to do.

Go Big, Go Redwood

The great John Muir said, "The clearest way into the Universe is through a forest wilderness."

Henry David Thoreau, Rachel Carson, Ralph Waldo Emerson, even Kerouac found a moment or two of bliss and respite from his internal madness out in the Big Sur wilderness. They all loved nature.

However, I am fairly certain that what these fine folks suggested, was that putting oneself into nature can have a very positive impact on the state of one's spiritual and emotional well-being. I don't believe that anywhere in their writing did they suggest actually putting the nature into our bodies, if you catch my drift.

Or maybe they were. Trees, in particular, are something special.

In the early and mid nineties, I became loosely involved with some regional environmental activism. I attended Earthfirst! meetings, read Green Anarchy literature, traveled hours to block logging roads, listened to Judi Bari speak and read my first-born **The Lorax** at least twenty times a day. I boycotted companies that owned stock in Pacific Lumber. I used cloth diapers that I washed myself. I switched my focus from psychology to environmental studies in community college. I started hanging out with a lot of pagans, anarchists and tree sitters. I left nasty notes on business's garbage bins if I saw recyclables piling over. I wasn't your typical treehugger, though; I usually sat out of the contact-love, opting instead to observe the misguided hippies embracing trees in the pouring rain, their large paper-mâché tree spirit puppets dissolving at their feet. Through it all, something about threatened old- growth redwoods, my role as a new parent and my disgust with the global corporate entity gave me a sense of purpose: to dismantle the whole system and, of course, to commune with the trees.

Despite my deep desire to really feel a connection to my environment, I like to remember myself as being fairly well adjusted and levelheaded during those days. I remained calm when loggers ripped my windshield wipers off my car, refused to sell me gas because of a small HEADWATERS FOREST sticker on my gas cap, and threw Molotov cocktails into my friend's camp site the night before a massive march.

None of it deterred me. If anything, all of it made me love the trees even more. I've always rooted for the underdog. Even if the underdog couldn't root for me.

But still, I could never support how some people took their love of trees to the next level. I'm not just referring to tree sitters ascending great heights into redwood canopies or the aforementioned inter species hugging bonanzas. I'm talking about people who have sexual relations with trees. It's been assumed that some of the overly open-minded and feral eco-erotics I often heard tales of were simply into objectum sexuality, were lonely, took too much acid and never fully returned to the reality or were picking up on some serious mojo from the redwoods that I was just too spiritually stunt-ed to receive. Regardless of the assorted motivating factors that shoved them into the tangled branches of desire, some people exposed their genitals to the unforgiving roughness of cold, scraggy bark.

Certainly, there is something magical about walking through a misty grove of coastal redwood trees. That is one of the reasons I love camping. A wild and crazy universal power has coaxed me, on occasion, to even spend days na-ked in the shadow of bristlecone pines. I've entertained ex-plicit fantasies of sexy- time with a sexy man in hidden hot springs that over look the vast Pacific. I've stripped naked in deserts (OK, that was the one time I went to Burning Man. And I was on drugs.). I've experienced surges of un-explained emotion when met with the beauty of wild flow-ers in the Irish countryside and had super fucking mystical experiences in a Central American mango grove and at the sheer sight of an acacia tree, standing solo in the savannah during a Kenyan sunset. And sure, I've nibbled a little soft redwood bark in order to integrate myself more deeply into nature while on a mushroom trip among old growth trees. Who hasn't?

But to form a sexual relationship to a tree, to marry a tree, to claim a tree as one's life partner–without a tree's written or verbal consent–despite my celebration of sexuality in all forms, is just plain creepy and weird.

Or is it?

Facing my own midlife crossroad, the thought of forming a relationship with a tree seemed something I shouldn't entirely dismiss. Though my priorities continue to shift, I still stand in solidarity with the trees. I'm still an adventurous spirit. And I'd still like a stable, reciprocal relationship based on mutual respect and common dreams. Also, low expectations, no pressure to meet family members (and hence no worrying about their disapproval), no dirty socks strewn about, no screaming matches late at night, it all held the appeal and temptation of an exotic, no-strings-attached love affair. With a tree, I thought, I'd always know what to expect. A tree couldn't cheat, lie, steal. I could move through the world without emotional constraints and he'd always be there. Standing tall and proud. Like a tree. Every attempt at relationships had failed. I needed to try something new, something so different than involving myself with the typical, emotionally unavailable men I usually fell for. I needed to open my heart to a tree.

I weighed the pros and cons: He won't go on road trips with me, he doesn't have a job, he can't swim and I'm pretty sure he doesn't cook. On the upside, he knows I am committed to his personal growth and well-being. He's very patient with my children, he's consistent, he's into bird watching and he can't run away at the first sign of conflict.

I figured, hey, I'll try anything once. And who knows? Maybe this new guy will grow on me. And we can grow together. It doesn't always have to be fireworks and tsunamis of passion from the get-go, right? It had to be one step above internet dating, right?

Instead of immediately giving up the goods and having sex with a partner that would likely leave splinters lodged into my thighs and abrasions in my nether region, I decided to take things slow with my potential life partner. I really wanted to get to know him first. I selected the large sycamore that lives outside my bedroom window, even though the redwood across the fence was my first choice. And although I know from experience that dating a neighbor isn't always the best idea, the sycamore and I have known each other for about eight years. I figure this is a good basis for something healthy and solid.

First, I approached him with apologies about the various nails I've hammered into his limbs. "The treehouse, the bird feeder, the rope swing, they are all embellishments that make you that much more appealing," I said. "Kind of like when I wear that earth tone scarf that you like so much."

Unresponsive, I assumed he was OK with the nails. He's so big and strong, I'm sure he wouldn't mind if I pounded, like, fifty more into his hefty, enduring body. He's solid. Like a tree should be.

Next, I asked if he'd like a massage. He didn't say yes but he also didn't protest, so I began slowly stroking his trunk. Having a background in massage therapy, I figured I'd try to work some of his knots out, help him relax. I applied lavender oil. He remained tense. I tried to open myself up to feeling the powerful energy that so many dendrophiliacs swear they feel pulsing through the bark and straight into their souls. The only energy I felt were waves of concern from my staring neighbors, surely convinced that I had lost my shit. I told him I'd see him the next day. This pattern repeated itself over the following weeks.

Though I grew fond of his deep listening skills, his attentiveness, one day I needed more than a good listener. I was all, "Hey, Tree. How are you doing today? I had a bad day and need a foot rub and maybe dinner, followed by some sexual healing."

He remained silent. Closed off.

"What's that? I can't hear you. Oh, you're not responding? Why are you ignoring me?!?"

We just stood there staring at one another, this tree and I. My mind haunted with memories of past relationships with humans, all of my insecurities crept up. I wasn't trying hard enough, I wasn't pretty enough, I was too needy. I could tell this tree was not a good match for me. I knew he'd never change. That we'd repeat this pattern over and over unless I chopped him down. He was bringing out the worst in me. He was too rigid. Too proud. Too distant.

"I don't think I can love someone or something that isn't going to love me back. Call me selfish, I've already had that experience," I cried. "Sycamore tree, it's over. I still want to be friends but this behavior is hurting me. And I think I have feelings for that redwood over there. I think he understands me. I think he'll meet my needs. I'm sorry, but this is how it has to be."

He really seemed to handle the break-up better than I did.

Looking back, I knew that I should have followed my friend's advice when he suggested: Go big, Dani. Go redwood. The silent treatment, the emotional unavailability, I deserved it all for settling for something convenient, something other than what I really desired, a sycamore instead of a redwood. And maybe the lack of sex hurt him as much as his silence hurt me. I should have sanded him, prepared him for physical love instead of shying away from splinters and demanding conversation when he wanted quiet time alone with me, for us to just hole one another.

We're working on a friendship, the sycamore and I. I'm healing and storing up the courage to approach the redwood. I've been his advocate, his friend for so many years. We've been through a lot over the years. I think he likes me, too and feels that we'd make a fine match.

At least that's what his body language tells me.

Bad Feminist

You can tell from her furry boots, her crocheted lavender half- shirt revealing her bronzed pierced navel and her glimmering bindi that she's super into Tantra and goddesses and shit. And you can tell that after about seven seconds of soul-staring straight into your boyfriend's eyes that he's really into Tantra and goddesses and shit now, too. Her hypnotic gaze makes it impossible for her to see you, standing right there, the cuff of your boyfriend's sleeve brushing against your wrist while she caresses his hand less than three inches away. But it doesn't matter that you're *right there.* She is so in tune with her womanly energy that any unspoken feminist code about women treating other women with respect has diminished in the face of sexual competition and her right to celebrate her divine Shakti-yoni power.

And this isn't the only way it happens. Women snub each

other in so many ridiculous ways. Gallery openings, protest marches, morning cafe rushes, craft fairs, fucking Tot Time with the kids at the local library. Women pick apart other women from head to toe or ignore them completely, even though they've met, like, seventeen times. And even though you are standing **right** fucking *there*.

"I'm married to a successful civil rights attorney and play in the New York Philharmonic. What do you do?"

"I know. We've met a few times. I'm a writer, remember? We met at that charity bike ride and–"

"You don't have the body of a cyclist at all. And you don't really look familiar. Have I read your work?"

"Probably not." *You're too amazing and a way better person than I am. You probably don't even need to read and just absorb knowledge and worldly wisdom through your perfectly tight pores or your extra- long eyelashes, you evil bitch. My out-of-shape body and I will just go home now and make a voodoo doll with the button I ripped off your purse while you were bragging about your perfect kids.*

Sometimes it's challenging to really like all women. I feel bad about that but I'm trying to be honest while I figure out a way around it.

I haven't always felt this way; the instant eye rolling, the seething resentment boiling up, clenching the inside of my face and pulling it down into the bitter, grotesque scowl of a citrus-sucking mongrel. The button-ripping, the witchery, that's all new, too. Sure, I've tossed around catty comments, dropped the word skank (I like how my jaw feels when I say it) and called a fair share of my fellow females crazy bitches over cocktails and phone calls and even hikes out in the great expanse of rolling hills and beachside trails that I wander through. I'm not proud of it. The words just roll out, second nature. Half of the time, I barely even think about what I'm saying.

I'm not quite sure when I really started noticing the snotty, competitive, insecure behavior between adult women or the moment when I started really despising certain members of this population. I remember it happening a lot in high school. I know a certain faction of my women-related annoyances germinated within circumstances involving said mean women in relation to a particular ex-boyfriend or three. I know I'd like to shake a big angry finger at the corporate media entity for constantly fueling the chick vs. chick fire. But I can't blame everyone else. You know, because, as they always say: one finger pointed away leaves a fist of cracked cuticle phalanges pointing straight back at one's miserable self. I'm a part of it, too.

I'm a bad feminist, a disenfranchised sister of the third wave, a baffled crusader of women's rights.

And I've been terribly naïve.

I thought, for a long time, that feminism wasn't strictly defined by listening to a lot of all-girl bands or whether or not a woman was independent enough to secure a high-powered position in a high-powered field of business. I've even been naïve enough to think that feminism means more than just the typical sexual liberation theories, granting all women everywhere the right to screw when and how and who they want. Aside from all of these pieces of the feminist puzzle,

I thought feminism's basic foundation meant living by the unspoken golden rules of solidarity and support we should offer each other as women, regardless of lifestyle choices, sexual orientation, race, hairstyle, level of yoga involvement, parental status, favorite color, geographic location. And by support, I mean, I thought we'd all be quite a bit nicer to one another, especially as we grow old and learn a few things from the fucked up patriarchal bullshit weighing us down, trying to enforce even more bullshit-laden, out-dated standards by which to live our lives and view or use our bodies.

But no. Women tearing other women apart has become a form of acceptable entertainment. Ladies wearing the same designer dress, pasted across the pages of magazines, compared, picked apart, given validation for surgically altered beauty or shredded to bits for celebrating their lovely, human-sized thighs or for having even two or three wrinkles. And sure, I suppose it can be argued that celebrities know what they are getting into when they make that transition from everyday human being to glamorous, other-worldly super star. Still, it grows increasingly more difficult to keep the judging and insecurities focused on those glossy pages. It shouldn't be there either, but it is. And it spills over in waves of ruthless cattiness and into the lives of the rest of us. It creates a bunch of real life bullies that are difficult to coexist with. This, in turn, makes women uncomfortable in their own skin, hyper- conscious of every millimeter of their pulsing organs, looking for others to lash out at or compete against to validate their place in this bitch-slapping world. *Every woman for herself. Pretty girls on the lifeboats first. Get the fuck out of my way.* In the worst case scenarios, women even start buying into the whole "blame the victim" tactic in serious issues of violence and assault. It's a mess.

I can't celebrate this part of being a woman. It's not empowering. It's not feminist. It makes me cringe.

Additionally, no amount of financial accomplishment, published erotic poetry, freaky tantric soul-staring or goddess-symbol tattoos make you a feminist if you're making your way in the world by consciously fucking over other women, and criticizing every piece of them, down to their shoe size or the color of their god damn yoga mat. It just doesn't work that way.

We're not in the dark ages. We won't be burned at the stake if we are kind to each other or protect each other.

And we *should* be kind to each other. And not with gifts or backhanded insults, but in sincere ways. We should pat each other on the back when we accomplish things instead of one- upping, dismissing or passive-aggressively bullying each other into feeling bad about achieving things. We should stop trying to bang each other's boyfriends or girlfriends. We should be able to celebrate our victories–both big and small–without worrying that it will alienate us. We have enough to deal with already without screwing each other over for men that nine times out of ten don't deserve us anyway. We don't need to throw each other under the bus just to prove that we can. That's what conservative right-wing politicians are for.

Not that we should go all Eeyore, hanging our heads and dismissing poor treatment from anyone–Oh *bother, she's a woman. I guess I'll be a feminist and show solidarity by not causing conflict*–that is not at all what I am suggesting. Nor do I believe that all women, everywhere should constantly engage in group hand massages or continuously stroking and braiding fresh-picked wild flowers into each other's hair in public. I just want us all to be nice to each other. And for us to all have each other's backs. And for us to stop comparing and dismissing. And for us to stop soul-staring each other's boyfriends. And for us to stop dating guys who succumb to soul stares. Especially when we're standing *right fucking there.*

It's the least we deserve.

Buying Time

It all started, much like most parents' fears, at the onset of my oldest daughter's puberty. Her hormones raged, mildly at first and then swelled into tsunami-like waves- ebbing and flowing like a madwoman, charging forward and then crawling away; ranting and then crying. Demanding milkshakes and turning away from my hugs. Her half-ass attempts at dressing for school turned into hours in the bathroom. Weekend mornings pleading for pancakes and cartoons were replaced with groggy breakfasts at noon... which were followed by extended naps behind closed doors. Then, came talk of boys- and then girls- and then boys again.

Throughout those oh-so-magical first years of puberty, a deep and desperate panic crept up from somewhere inside of me. As I caught our reflections passing by a window one morning, I realized that my sweet little girl, who once nestled herself to sleep in my arms and came running and sobbing with skinned knees and gravel-embedded palms is not a little girl anymore. At all. Instead of climbing on my shoulders to see through the crowds we sometimes find ourselves in, she stands nearly eye-to-eye with me, wearing my clothes and make-up. As a parent, I have accepted and even come to cherish the constant changes in my kids and the stages of development they weave in and out of. But I also more-recently realized, with much less confidence, that someday in the not so distant future, this little girl who is quickly becoming a woman is going to fall in love, have sex and quite likely going to have her heart-broken.

Now, upon this realization, all of my self-righteous ideas of raising strong, ass-kicking, take-no-shit, tough-as-nails, sexually-liberated feminist daughters immediately switched to fear and dissipated. I managed to keep my anxiety under-wraps for the most part and expressed it casually at first, with my sweaty palms shoved firmly into my pockets. I'd hint, nonchalantly, that "eh- boys, shmoyz: you've got the rest of your life to deal with them. They actually take a lot of time and patience to deal with. You should focus on your art and get your math grades up first. Spend more time with your friends instead of worrying about them." Eventually, however, I found myself desperate with a sense of control that I had never imagined and began, with much neurosis and embarrassment, to offer my sweet teenage daughter, cold hard cash to avoid relationships all together.

First, I dished out an offer of $100 to not kiss a boy until she turned 16. Easy enough, I thought. I could buy her obedi-ence, right? Super easy with teens, right? Next, I stepped it up a notch and offered her $300 if she waited until she was

18 and suggested an increase in funds if she could hold it together through the following years of college. My worst nightmare was for her to let the Twilight series inform her world and have her get all wrapped up in a co-dependent relationship with a whiny, starving emo vampire guy or some aggressive, angry werewolf guy (no matter how sweet his abs are). So I pushed the money her way. Her response, complete with the stereo-typical "are you fucking kidding me?" teenager facial expression only fueled my inner madness as she began making counter- offers, "well, if I do get a boyfriend and start kissing and stuff, then, like, I guess I'll just give you some money, ok mom?"

I was screwed. I talked to friends and listened to advice, which made me feel mostly better. Then, I rehashed my own behavior during my teenage years, which really did nothing other than motivate me to find chastity belts and chains to lock her up with. Finally, after much obsessing, I understood that I had to let it go. More importantly, I realized that I couldn't afford or justify forking out cash for something so ridiculous when what she really needs are braces and a new pair of shoes. But I did arrive at a place of really understanding my motives around this issue. Becoming this dreadful, overprotective mother would essentially rob my daughter from experiences she needs to have to become the amazing woman that I know she is. I'd be robbing her of all of the fun and magic and awkwardness of first kisses and late night phone calls and eventually giggly girl-talk over rug burns and tear-jerking, soul-shaking passion.

As I began to loosen my death grip on her, I also faced my own issues. What I was trying to do, mostly on a subconscious level but also because I am mildly nuts, was to buy my own way out of the hurt and abuse and soul-crushing heart-ache I had fallen victim to. As parents, we will quite often go to ridiculous lengths to protect our kids and I found that I was a willing and eager warrior set out to battle against some mythical future that I hadn't even caught a glimpse of. I never want her to worry about whether or not she is good enough for some guy. I don't want her second-guessing her-self or believing that she should change to accommodate someone else's media- influenced beauty standards. What I lost sight of in focusing in on the troubles I've seen, are the kisses that cause knees to shake and go limp, late night whispers, the adventurous thrills of vacation sex, Sunday afternoon rendezvous with secret lovers, and the empower-ment that comes along with allowing pleasure and connec-tion with people in our lives.

I know I can't protect my girls from everything, despite a natural mama bear instinct that wells up inside at just the thought of them shedding even a single tear. What I can do-and should do, is continue to encourage and empower them by example. The best I can do is to be honest and available and show them that I am worthy of the love and passion that sometimes comes my way. This will hopefully pave the roads with confidence, regardless of which direction they take. I also know that I need to let them live their own lives while I balance between stepping back and opening my arms to them when they need to come crying, cracked hearts and bruised egos. And, just as a back-up plan I have stashed that $100 bill away in a Swiss bank account in case my new found humility ever takes a back seat.

One Settled Comfortably In
The Cuckoo's Nest

No one wants to talk about Uncle Bob's chronic depression or why it is that Aunt Sue refuses to travel anywhere by boat. Grandpa's electric shock therapy and Grandma's time in the state mental hospital are seldom the focus of conversation. On rare occasions, a distant cousin will hint to some less-than- glamorous faction of family history after one too many wine spritzers at the annual family reunion. A new, married-into- the-family member will allude to the fact that *someone* has "issues," the comment delivered with a tinge of sarcasm, as humor is always easier to stomach than the cold hard truth that some of us come, quite frankly, from families of wackos.

What's worse than acknowledging this history, is admitting

to yourself and the loved ones nearby, that some level of mental illness has quite possibly set up shop inside of us as well. Some insist that we're just not trying enough alternative remedies to cure whatever ails us. Something's wrong? Fix it! Immediately! Buy something! Or let go of attachments! Change your outlook on life! Manifest the happiness thatresides within! You need a detox diet! Smudge your bedroom with sage! You create your own reality! We're all supposed to be happy! Everything is so good! We can manifest joy! Try harder!

Sure, some people are "cured" with didgeridoo sound healings, 5-HTP supplements and tapping all over their faces while chanting positive affirmations. That is super great for them, as they are likely not suffering from the gnarly chronic depression and anxiety I'm referring to. For some of us, color therapy and yoga don't make it go away.

Not that we don't try. Some of us try everything because we're afraid of being judged by our "liberal, do-good" communities if we take medication. We undergo hypnotherapy, past life regression, tarot readings. We visit shamans and get acupuncture treatments. We'll become cyclists, participating in every 100-mile ride we can find, attempting to outride whatever keeps grasping at us with it's viscous claws. We do eight million sun salutations. We drive two days through the desert to see the Dalai Lama. We borrow our friends' light therapy boxes, eat mounds of Omega-3 fatty acid-rich food. Sometimes we give up and eat two pounds of bacon in a weekend. We'll churn our own butter and stand alone in the kitchen devouring it by the spoonful before smearing it onto chocolate cake that we often consume while soaking in the bathtub, reading Pema Chödrön, listening to Iron and

Wine. Crying. Defeated. Our ulcers hurt.

After a break up, we're expected to cut our hair and pull on a new tight-fitting red dress to chase away any residual sadness with a series of one-night stands. If we lose a job, it's off to happy hour to pound back some pints, listen to jokes and head on our way to Craigslist where we send countless résumés off with the naïve optimism of new liberal arts graduates. If a loved one dies, we get two to three bereavement days–if we're lucky–to pick up the pieces, get the kids to school on time, drag ourselves back to the office and start filing, making non-fat lattes for underweight women or returning to classrooms full of screaming preschoolers. We smile while finger-paint gets smeared down our legs. "It'll be good for you to be back at work," our well-meaning friends say. "You need to move on."

And aside from the situational depression or anxiety we're all plagued with when relationships end, loved ones die, or our homes foreclose, some of us are just wired differently. We have stunted nervous systems. Miswired synapses. Surges of imbalanced chemicals. Physical and emotional trauma that we never really get over. Even when the sun shines its glorious brightness on our faces, the bills are paid and the people in our lives really, really love us, some of us can't help it. It's not that we are ungrateful. We just hurt. A lot.

On top of whatever predispositions we're born with, maybe something horrible happened to us. Maybe we have chronic health issues. Maybe someone we thought would be here forever suddenly died. Maybe we thought it was our fault. Maybe we visited a place so dark that we couldn't see anything but the trauma or our loved one's absence and maybe when we came back, part of that place stuck to us like a layer of soot across our eyes. Or an iron weight in our throat. A shadow that filters how we feel and think about the world, tinging everything with shades of gray.

And we don't want to talk about it. Or we do, but we're afraid to.

Some may fear that talking about our long-standing relationships with mental illness may set up road blocks.

We're afraid that if we tell our lovers something awful that someone did to us–and how it affected us–that they won't touch us anymore. *And oh my God, we need to be touched.* We're afraid we'll lose our friends, our jobs, our families. We're worried that our depression or anxiety or PTSD or struggles with addiction will become scapegoats for someone else's bad choices. If we're women, we are viewed as crazy, hormonal bitches. If we're men, we need to "man up" and stop being pussies. If we are children, we just get lost.

So we stay home and cry on the floor of our daughter's bedroom and listen to Elliot Smith for hours when we find out someone we love killed himself. We spend days alone in the woods with a bag of pumpkin seeds and Emergen-C packets after we watch our friend die of cancer. Some of us cut ourselves. Some of us overeat. Some of us starve ourselves. We poison ourselves with substances of every sort. We do these things because we don't think we deserve better. Or we don't know how to stop. We'll switch our phones off, turn out the lights and crawl under dirty sheets with tiny bottles of essential oils, just waiting for what feels like a blizzard of shit to pass. Waiting and waiting and waiting, sometimes hating ourselves for not feeling "normal" and for feeling too much about everything, all of the time.

Sometimes we take lovers who we know will break our hearts as more often than not, we're attracted to the same dark madness that we see in ourselves. And sometimes we try really, really hard to have "normal" relationships with "normal" people who have no idea who we are inside. And we'll feel guilty about who we are and we'll think–and even believe–that we're not good enough so sometimes we'll sabotage it because being alone, watching documentaries about Darfur every weekend is more comforting than admitting who we are.

Sometimes, some of us will make the most of it. *I will write such great poetry when I come out of this.* And we'll overindulge. We might start smoking because it seems dark and sexy, even though it makes our stomachs hurt, and we'll sit on the front porch alone, with a cigarette, a bottle of Chianti and a bowl of kalamata olives, coughing, watching the sun sink, the muffled sound of recorded violins drifting out a nearby window. Sunset and empty wine bottle as metaphors. Unbearable loneliness pressed against our chests. Sometimes we'll believe we're on a mystical spiritual journey. Maybe we are. Who even knows what that means?

And the truth is, we don't all make it. Some of us will relapse, overdose and die. Some of us will drink too much and never wake up. Some will drive off of cliffs. Some of us will take too many pills or use a gun or a knife. Some of us will check into a hospital and never come out. This will chip at us and we'll feel guilty that we're still here. Our bodies transform into glass. Already cracked, we hold onto fear of catching one last pebble that will drop us, shattering us to glossy bits across the floor.

"Is this where I am heading? What if I can't find my way out of this? What if I end up like her? Like him? Dead?"

We're all–us, the chronically depressed and anxiety-ridden–thinking it, though no one will say it out loud.

For the lucky ones, we learn to adapt and stockpile an arsenal of tools to help us get through the black holes that become regularly featured guests in our lives. We settle comfortably into a cuckoo's nest. It's a part of us. If we have money, we fly to Belize and smoke weed on sailboats. Or we stay home and get help in the form of therapists and pills and good food and learn to turn down the inner voice that tells us we suck. When that doesn't work, we learn to call our friends. When our friends aren't home, we learn to call hotlines or take meds or hold it together until the kids go to bed and then sit in the dark and let our minds go to bad places, remembering that we've been there before and its OK to visit as long as we have some sort of road map to lead us back. We watch **Fight Club** and **Children of Men** and soothe ourselves with David Attenborough-narrated ocean documentaries while clinging to hot water bottles in order to feel warmth–tricking our minds into believing we're not alone. Then we crawl into bed with our kids, holding their tiny hands while they sleep. Their breath keeps us from unraveling.

Sometimes we blast Public Enemy and Crimpshrine and scream. We tear everything off of the walls and paint them red. Or Green. Or gray. We read somewhere that changing our environment can change our moods. We'll break shit and burn things and chop wood or take a mandolin that we can't even play and sit and watch our chickens scratch and peck at leftover salad. And we'll cry.

We still try to help each other, delivering tacos by bike, driving each other to doctors and funerals and the unemployment office. We'll send inappropriate texts to make each other laugh out loud at work or on the bus. We sleep on kitchen floors with each other while we wait for inevitable bad news to come. We cook together and for each other and never turn away.

And, if we're really fortunate, we can wipe some soot from our eyes and see it all as a twisted and necessary gift. Not like a new watch or a first edition autographed copy of our favorite novel, mind you, but a gift nonetheless, one that gives us the super power of loving with the passion of fifty sex-crazed poets. One that helps us find more than cracked sand dollars and polished glass as we sift through sand at the beach. One that reminds us how incredible and beautifully disastrous life is when the shadow lifts for that month or year and we can smile again and all of our depressed friends think we are total fuckers.

We know it will come back, like an audit or a flat tire late at night–unexpectedly, ruthlessly–so we enjoy the sunshine while it lasts.

Our therapists say we're doing OK, that we are actually coping quite well in our cuckoo's nest.

And one day, with what feels like scratching the silver from a winning lottery ticket, we'll wake up and actually believe it's true.

I'm Dreaming Of An Anne Frank Christmas

I've never really been a fan of Christmas. The religious-themed music, car-clogged parking lots, the screeching children strapped in faux velvet and dangerously tight hair ribbons waiting to see Santa; all of it makes me incredibly uneasy. I suppose that growing up in a working-class home with nearly a dozen people plagued with varying degrees of psychosocial challenges–and receiving mid-December birthday gifts packaged in Santa-slathered wrapping paper–might lead the best of us into developing an aversion to Baby Jesus' birthday. Through the years my own aversion grew quite strong, eventually settling into something like resentment.

For me, Christmas was never delivered in the shiny, neatly wrapped box with a snow-dusted Rudolf frolicking around outside, or familial holiday cheer like CBS holiday specials and the infamous ***Peter Comes Home for Christmas*** Folger's commercial falsely implied. No relatives visited. Our family never attended holiday church services. And although I have faint memories of stacking my plate with chewy slabs of ham and watching the box wine squeeze out its last drops of sour medicine for my parents, there were no formal dinners. I don't blame my parents. They were poor with too many kids, and too tired to erupt into holiday cheer when Christmas was likely looked at as a much needed day home from work. I blame the marketing industry.

Still, the holidays were quite simply a disappointment, with the worst factor playing out after the return to school a week or so later. Classmates flocked to an icy playground to take inventory of who wore sweet new puffy moon boots or who spent the two-week break sipping hot chocolate in between runs down snow-packed mountain slopes at various Sierra ski resorts. The schoolyard also played host to a holiday candy trade of sorts featuring hot list items, like Lifesavers Christmas Storybooks or giant Hershey's Kisses encased in masses of dazzling red foil, neither of which I'd received. I would lie, explaining to my peers that I had already devoured my heaps of fanciful treats. In reality, my stocking brimmed with bitter, hard-shelled mixed nuts and oranges too sour for my prepubescent taste buds.

Christmas, in short, was a letdown of phenomenal proportions. I felt strongly that "The First Noel" could suck it.

Years later, at the onset of adulthood, I found myself delivering my first born on Christmas Eve. Given my unconventional leanings, I had hoped she'd emerge closer to her due date on winter solstice, shortly after the doctors had induced me with an intravenous drip of Pitocin. Several days and undisclosed amounts of Demerol and morphine later, she was forced out of the womb and into the second verse of "O Holy Night" sung by carolers and hospital staff roaming the hallways of the maternity ward. Suddenly, something changed. I'm sure there is a possibility that the post-childbirth hormones rushing through my bloodstream clouded my judgment, but in those first few moments of holding my wrinkly little elf of a daughter, my resentment toward poinsettias and holly jolly Jesus lovers softened a bit. My inner cynic was silenced for at least forty-five minutes.

The arrival of new motherhood brought with it pressure to provide my kids with every unfulfilled holiday fantasy I watched slip by during my own childhood. At first, I pushed forward, determined to recreate my very own Northern California version of the Family Ties' Christmas specials. I overcompensated by piling gifts of handmade wooden block sets, fair trade crayons and politically correct coloring books under our live solstice-slash-Christmas-slash-birthday tree. Eventually, a dwindling income and anticlimactic post holiday letdown called for simplifying and managing resources with sporadic "life lesson" elements mixed in. I figured, fuck it; if I am growing humans in the science lab of my womb with the expectation that they'll eventually blossom into walking, talking members of society, I better create something unique and memorable for them. The last thing the world needs are more kids flippantly plowing through heaps of child-labor produced, phthalate-soaked plastic crap that will just crumble in a month's time anyway.

I set out with an agenda. And this agenda was not strictly limited to winter holiday madness.

In the springtime, May Day was often spent dancing around

flowery trees or marching through our neighborhood in support of labor and immigrants' rights. Throughout the summer, family camping trips were often planned in conjunction with tree sits in groves of old-growth redwood trees. October was usually saturated with lessons of the religious crusades, reminding my girls of the origins of Halloween and how completely insulting it is for the general public to demonize witches when, historically, witches were just trying to make shit right. That was followed closely by Dia de Los Muertos events, our growing altar bursting with photos of loved ones. Thanksgiving was observed as Indigenous People's Day beginning with a sunrise ceremony commemorating the 1969 occupation of Alcatraz, followed with a homemade wine guzzling potluck with friends where I could sometimes be found reading passages of **Lies My Teacher Told Me** to any and every young and impressionable child who would listen.

Regardless of our (i.e., my) political holiday agenda, the kids have been indoctrinated into remembering that regardless of how bad things might be for us at times, everyone else has it much much worse, the lingering sound of my voice surely the source of many late night anxiety attacks: *Never forget the suffering of others. Never. Forget.*

But somewhere in between righteous activism and the rancid taste of defeat, I began backing away from confronting the iron fist of capitalism. I still correct disparaging language and certainly point out differences between the haves and the have-nots when the time calls. But in my darkest, most Christmas-is-oppressive-bah-humbug moments, I sometimes fear that all that is wrong with our society is so cemented into place that there is little chance of humanity's survival, so I go ahead and look the other way. I'm not apathetic, really. Just like my own parents were during holidays past, I'm just incredibly tired. Plus my Seasonal Affective Disorder isn't much of a remedy for my inner Grinch.

So, when recently participating in the soft-pedaled political agenda I call "story time," my youngest daughter, filled with her larger than average eleven-year-old heart, looked up at me, each eye a dazzling, sparkling blue and each freckle a kiss straight from God's own personal and devoted angel servants. Having just turned the page of Anne Frank's diary entry of celebrating Christmas in the secret annex with gifts of bread and pencils, my daughter's face brightened.

"Mama, I want to have an Anne Frank Christmas this year," she proclaimed with hope for a better world—a world of magic and wonderment—clinging to each and every syllable.

I was dumbfounded.

After the initial horror of what could be easily seen as an inappropriate statement from a privileged little white girl passed, I realized that my awkward attempts at reclaiming the holidays had an effect—an awkward one, but an effect, nonetheless.

She wasn't suggesting that we burrow into the walls and attic of our little home to nosh on a diet of dried peas and fear. She knows I just don't have the energy or resources to embark on a complete remodel of our rental. Nor was she glamorizing human tragedy, in which the victims of war and violence are too often young children. I've applied guilt—disguised as humility—in such thick coats that it has become a permanent, many layered shell of reality for my kids; she would never participate in an abominable World War II reenactment.

I think she recognized, in that moment, that simplicity is where it's at.

Like my own longing, which led me to dig deep through holidays and traditions choked to the gills with consumer-driven emptiness, this sweet kid just wants to find meaning in a world that has allowed the holidays to be turned into a Jerry Springeresque spectacle. Pepper spray and stampede incidents through discount stores all in the name of obtaining some flimsy, sweatshop produced, overly packaged nonsense have replaced generosity and tenderly shared moments that this god damn holiday season is supposed to offer. Even for those of us who would rather avoid Celine Dion Christmas music or have birthdays painfully close to the holidays, deep down we all just want our lives trimmed with magic and sweetness.

In the end, there is nothing that any of us can do to avoid the build-up to Santa time, whether our belief systems call us to celebrate or not. Red and green window paintings flocked with toxic faux snow are shellacked across businesses as early as Columbus Day, the calluses and flip-flops of summer barely behind us. Sale ads jam our mailboxes, reminding us to start buying shit that no one really even wants or needs, because that's what Christmas now represents for far too many people. The best that any of us can do is to is recreate the holidays and reclaim them for our own, even if that means dressing in moth-nibbled wool and scribbling lists of our hopes and dreams in our diaries by beeswax candlelight.

For my daughters and me, our two-foot tall faux redwood

stands perched beside our paper snowflake lined window, white lights–very likely manufactured by tiny hands in an asbestos clouded factory warehouse, but whatever–flicker from its branches. As per tradition we'll eat cookies and eggs for breakfast and play John Prine's *Christmas in Prison* on repeat for at least an hour before feasting and laughing with our most cherished friends. And adding to the tradition this year, we'll read a little Anne Frank and bake bread with the sourdough starter my wee one put on her modest holiday wish list.

And deep inside, under layers of sweatshirts and bathrobes and maybe a mild hangover from the previous night's soynog and brandy, I'll be secretly hoping that all of the weird shit I force onto my innocent children won't make them grow up to hate me. Instead, I hope they look back and think that maybe Christmas isn't so bad. And that maybe, Mom and her recovering bleeding heart necrosis finally got what it's all about.

If You Like Pina Coladas

Dating is a mess. It can sometimes feel as if a big gob of conflicting and tentacled emotions have attached to us, twisting their ways around the mechanisms of common sense, squeezing out any rational thought. We humans can sometimes confuse that inner fluttering of intuition–telling us to run–for something more like the excitement that comes in those first stages of love. We confuse sudden increases in libido with loneliness and seek out relationships when all we need is a quick and satisfying roll in the proverbial hay. We make assumptions and demands, ask too many questions right away and very often end up disillusioned.

Online dating is supposed to make this all easier. Lists of deal-breakers and quirks and expectations should filter out those who are better suited far away from us, in places like frat houses, jail, NRA conventions, church. Accompanying photographs show us whether the person is tall enough, stylish enough, happy enough, adventurous enough or creative enough to take out in public or to procreate with. Online dating should be awesome. But really, it's not.

After years of reluctance around answering personals in the back pages of my local alt-weekly while humming the desperately awful "Piña Colada/Escape" song, I finally embarked on my first blind date years ago with a guy I met through Friendster.

Joe, as I'll call him here (because I can't actually remember–or have mentally blocked–his name) lived in Berkeley, owned his own house, collected art and was well-traveled. Most importantly, he had good politics and was easy on the eyes. He could construct clever sentences and our online correspondence was lively and interesting. Our first phone conversation was brief, as we decided we'd save all of the "good stuff" for our coffee date the following week.

We met in a nearby town that neither of us frequently visited. As I walked into the cafe I knew in an instant that we weren't a match. All of my hopeful expectations disintegrated as he immediately launched a verbal attack against his ex-girlfriend, non-vegans and old people, while complaining of his hearing loss; the result of too many nights behind the turntable at Oakland raves. His whole body had a mild shake to it, a possible side effect of his high volume caffeine consumption or his unprocessed rage toward the world. "Now that I don't drink anymore, I am pretty miserable and tend to over-caffeinate," he scowled. Dude never smiled. He never made eye contact. And he didn't even open the door for me as we walked out to say goodbye on the street.

"Look, if you're not interested that's fine, I don't care. Just don't lead me on and play games," he warned in a tone that was a little intense for a first date. I'm pretty sure he had body parts in the trunk of his car.

I never saw or heard from Joe again.

Viewing my date with Joe as a fluke, as just one weathered stepping stone on my path to love, I put myself out there again. And again.

Interested in dating outside the incestuous circle of my smallish town, my naïvety and I moved on to seeking potential matches in other cities through the more straightforward and expansive world of Craigslist. I'd answer ads after using very specific search words like "activism", "reading", "travel", "PJ Harvey". And as a general rule I would avoid any post with 420, FWB, XBOX,STD or "Asian under 25yo ONLY" etched somewhere into the headline. I also hid from men who posted NO DRAMA OR GAMES in their ad titles, as the ads were not only poorly written but often contained self-portraits snapped in seedy hotel bathrooms or photos of shirtless, waxed, yolked-up bros flexing next to red Kawasakis. This, of course is fine for some women. I just tend to prefer my men a tad bit less douchey and maybe posing with a book, rescue animal or on assignment withNational Geographic instead. Also, for my own physical well-being, I avoid the intense cologne situation I assume these guys have going on. I also steer clear of NSA, which is not short forNASA scientist. What it really means is, A) Lives with parents so you can't sleep over, or B) Lives with girlfriend/ wife so you can't sleep over.

A friend experienced in online dating reminded me that on

the other end of the spectrum, men who say they are into "healthy living" usually show up at a first date wearing orange Turkish birthing pants. And beaded vests. Craigslist has no happy medium.

Aside from skimming the Men Seeking Women section and exploring my interest in dating women (I was usually only contacted by men named Chad and Robbie who wanted to watch two women having sex), I even cruised through the Missed Connections section. You know, sometimes I'd get "the eyes" at a bar or bookstore or something and I'd look to see if said flirt was missing me. But, as I've learned through the years, no one ever posts Missed Connections that read:

Seeking the funny, smart mom with confusing hair, carrying two pounds of nutritional yeast and a case of coconut water through Oliver's Market while arguing with her children about her decision to purchase the non-dairy ice cream instead of the carton of Breyers that they wanted. I bet you have a great personality. Let's chat!

So, despite Eddie Murphy's rendition of Buckwheat's "Wookin Pa Nub" tapping in the back of my mind, reminding me of the absurdity of what I was doing, I moved on to the big leagues.

Joining OK Cupid felt like cracking open a big, wonderful piñata packed full of new and spectacular party favors. The site was bursting with men and women from all walks of life, paired together with their most compatible matches through some kind of genius, super power rating system. The search engine allows users to seek out potential mates within specific parts of the world, within specific age ranges and even lets users select height, astrological signs and income range to weed out the crazy Scorpios, Capricorns and Pisces in the mix.

At first, the possibilities seemed endless. There was the writer who I became good friends with. The radical political science professor who took my friend and I out for drinks and dancing. The MIT graduate turned chef with great taste in music who burned me the perfect hip-hop mixed CD. And my personal favorite, the celibate South Asian vegan Buddhist film maker who I think I accidentally married at an ashram while receiving rose water blessings and hugs from my guru.

Our first date consisted of meeting at a natural food store to nosh on wheat-free organic treats from its cafe before moving on to skip rocks along a remote southern tip of the San Pablo Bay. Last I heard, he was expelled from a monastery, planning to sell his few belongings in order to move to a secluded island north of Japan, where he would bake bread and isolate himself from the temptations of the material world. We made a pact on our platonic wedding night, he and I: we will never taint our bond by marrying atheists or republicans.

It was all fun and games in the beginning. Then things went downhill, fast.

Aside from the awkwardness of spotting exes or friends on OK Cupid, there was the ex-boyfriend who created a fake profile, contacting me up to five times in a twelve-hour period in order to coax me into... *something*. The really angry, high-needs single dad who wrote me a scathing email when I didn't take his call while at work. The jerk who called me an ugly, self-involved bitch–via text message–for canceling our date to stay home with my sick kid. Another Buddhist-slash-intellectual with no sense of humor who constantly told me how much he hated white people. And the endless string of men who'd solicit dates while posting pictures of recent romantic vacations with their girlfriends on their Facebook pages (note to dudes: we all have access to Google). They all appeared flawless on OK Cupid's big pink screen. Yet aside from most of them being gainfully employed as college professors or artists, the common thread woven tightly through them all was the serious lack of commitment. I'm not just talking commitment as in none of them wanted to move in with me and raise my kids and pay my bills, I'm talking about the constant flakiness, the inability to make a decision about where to meet, the consistent blowing off, changing plans or canceling at the last minute. And the double dipping! If your significant other doesn't know, you can't call it polyamory!

I know, I know, men have complaints, too! What I've learned is that aside from lipstick-smeared duckfaces, one male friend says his biggest peeve is that most of the women claiming to be down to earth are the neediest, most high maintenance chicks out there. Also, men aren't usually looking for a "partner in crime".

"But the fun and appeal of online dating," says yet another male friend at a recent impromptu online dating roundtable discussion, "is that its not supposed to work!"

Despite knowing a small handful of couples who have found their little sweetie coochie-coos online, I think that maybe this friend is right. Maybe just like everything else in my generation, online dating is just one of the many avenues through which to fulfill a quick, insecurity-fed need for validation. *OMG he totally OK Cupid-winked at me! I'm pretty! Or I've got so many chicks online, dude, you don't even fucking KNOW.* Maybe it's just there for the countless thousands of newly single men and women to find easy rebound sex. Or maybe it's a combination of things. Throwing all of the eligible members of the annoyingly laid back west coast Slacker Generation into a website that feels like a big, silly video game full of sex questions might simply intensify the already apathetic, non-committal vibe that any of these factors alone are already saturated with. It's too much gunk to wade through, too many crossed signals to pick apart and interpret, too many greasy dudes on Kawasakis and not enough smarties cozied up with helpless little rescue animals.

Or maybe, quite possibly, it's just me.

Like a Born-Again Almost 40-Year-Old Virgin

I never imagined I'd practice celibacy. Never, ever in any of my wildest *I should become a Buddhist nun and crawl into a Nepalese cave forever* escapist fantasies did I even consider that I would ever stop having sex. I am telling you this; never, ever did I think it.

But it happened. A long time ago. My nights spent with emotionally unavailable men and the Xanax needed to sleep near them have been bartered for novels, battery-operated devices and lavender eye pillows. And ice cream. In some communities, I think this means I'm a virgin. Again.

I know for many monks and plane crash survivors stranded on icebergs and Catholic girls with surgically attached chastity belts, a year without sex is no biggie. Countless others practice intentionally sex-free lifestyles for even longer. But for me, it is different. I have carried this dark secret like a heavy, forked iron tail through my land of milk and honey, my land of sexual liberation, of casual sex and militant polyamory. Of BDSM clubs, sex parties, sacred sexuality workshops and Tantra conventions.

Being celibate in the Bay Area may be the biggest taboo of them all.

Of course, like most paths I've dragged myself down, I didn't exactly plan to move in this direction. Slimy boyfriends, one fruitless date after another, too many afternoons riding public transportation; it all wore me out. I grew tired of men treating me like some foul thing clinging to the bottom of their shoes. And so many years of choosing substandard men for myself short-circuited my intuition and clobbered what little sense of self worth I had to begin with. I stopped trusting myself. So I have closed up the girly bits shop, slipped on an invisible but highly effective magic chastity belt and dimmed my magical pelvic chakra glow until further notice.

Yes. I have other reasons.

And yes, it is possible that I've exhausted all of my available sexual resources in the small community I call home. I was once an enthusiastic one-woman welcome wagon, inviting men eagerly into the neighborhood of my bedroom. This, I cannot deny.

But I'm no longer a fresh spring lilac propped up all perky and sweet and luscious, covered in dew and nectar, just waiting for some stealthy and sexually ambitious bumble bee to pollinate the woman in me. It's not perimenopause; I'm on strike. My friends in Sex and Love Addicts Anonymous call it emotional anorexia. I call it exhaustion. I no longer possess the impulsive twenty-something gusto it takes to stay up all night engaging in the lengthy conversations that often lead to bad sex, regrets and cortisol imbalance. I know I've obviously missed the *fall in love young and start a writer slash artist slash organic farm compound and keep bees together and into the sunset forever* boat. I also think that maybe I don't need that. Or that I have everything I really need with my kids and my cats and my lemon balm and my generous hens and my bike and my lovely friends. And my aforementioned battery operated devices.

Sex and love are two separate creatures, you say? I shouldn't be so picky, you say?

While this is true, I need to be honest and state that I don't trust my oxytocin. You know that hormone that releases when women have sex and it makes us attach ourselves like so many high quality strips of flypaper to even the most unsuitable sociopaths we roll through the sheets with? It really does do tricky things to the body and mind. I know. I've attached myself to all sorts of gross people. Now I have a lot of it built up. If I'm letting that shit loose, it needs reprogramming first–like a behavioral boot camp for out-of-control, slutty teenage girls. It needs life vests and how-to guides. And maybe a deserving recipient.

And that's not all.

The biggest truth of it is, once, not long ago, I lost someone I loved. It did this thing to my insides that happens when you love someone so much that you believe he is your soul mate. And you have this child together who is so magical and beautiful that you could just tear her apart and eat her every last freckle. But he, this man you love so much, is also an addict. And against any molecule of better judgment you try to save him but you can't. So you try to save yourself and leave him and then sleep in your car with your kids and everything is gone and then you hate this man who you felt you already spent forever with. Then he begs for you to come back and makes you mixed CDs with sad, come-back-to-me Morrissey songs on every last one and you know he loves you so much but you're so angry and you say no, no, no. And you try to move on–sometimes with little baby steps like putting the things he left behind into boxes in the laundry room and sometimes with grand gestures like leaving the country. You still think of him every day and one day, when you stop hating him and you've become friends again, you say no to him one last time. And he dies; a suicide. It shoots a hundred arrows into every softest part of you. You leave the arrows there and they gather scar tissue in masses and knots and a piece of you–maybe a big piece of you–thinks you deserve all of the wounds that replace the softness you once had. And then, like a dumbass, you think that if you can only find someone else to love you, they will pull the knots out and carve the chunks of tough leathery scars away and put something good in their place.

It did that to me. It changed me in those ways. It destroyed a lot of those important soft parts, the soft parts that made me trust and love myself.

So I took the only logical next step I could take. I found some awful men and expected them to love me or have decent sex with me when they were not capable. I gasped *savemesavemesaveme* or *punishmepunishmepunishme* or *lovemelovemeloveme* because I thought that is what I needed to save myself.

For fuck's sake. It was so stupid. Too many John Hughes films, I'm afraid.

So I've taken time to sort out my brain and now, with this new weird virginity thing, I am remembering my soft parts. The parts of me that deserve all good things. All good people. All good laughter and love and amazing bright skies and warm water and things that make me sigh big long sighs of all things good.

And the intuition that I believed was still deeply embedded in the bottom of an ex-boyfriend's shoe is back. It is back and growing in me like an endangered poisonous creature from the Amazon River–dagger-like fins, circling and flipping and jumping in my gut when I stand too close to someone who is not right for me. I have to catch my breath, step back, sometimes run and hide and cover my mouth to keep the Devil Fish from swimming out with a great force, frothy gunk spewing from my face. It works. I no longer sleep with creeps.

But still.

Still, I think sometimes it would be quite nice–fucking *fantastic, really*–to find someone who will do a different thing, that thing that spring does with the cherry trees. In the least, it would be nice to find someone who doesn't make that Amazonian Devil Fish spin around so fast in my gut. My Own Private Devil Fish-slaying Neruda. *Wouldn't it be fucking fantastic?*

But I'm not so naïve these days. My soft parts remind me that the next guy I decide to play Bedroom Welcome Wagon with will have issues. All sorts of issues with varying degrees of seriousness like a gambling addiction and a mean dad and bad breath and a crazy bitch ex. *There are so many crazy ex girlfriends out there!* He may even have a bag of kitten heads or a collection of melted Barbie legs that he incorporates into weird Russian refugee role-play or taxidermy mice tucked into the back of his closet. Or seventeen underage girlfriends. None of it surprises me anymore.

But, the soft parts! How exciting to welcome their return. Together with the Devil Fish, I think these things will lead me to good sex. Or at least the desire to attempt sex again, which is slowly growing in me as well.

For example:

Recently, on a crisp and lovely San Francisco evening, I found myself surrounded by flowers and dinosaurs and warmth and big fancy words and a male friend leaned in to take my photograph and told me I looked nice and bought me a beer and I thought, take me with you. Anywhere. I imagined our bodies clutched together on his motorcycle–a very Prince and Apollonia fantasy, I know, except this friend is tall and blond and I am short and thirty-eight and could never pull of Apollonia's sexy spandex body suits. I imagined the two of us riding to some sketchy barn in a remote coastal apple orchard and so many fun things happening there.

Later, we swam instead. We filled the air and the fog and the cold of the lake and mosquito ears with all good laughter and all good things. Nowhere did I see, hear or feel a Devil Fish.

And though he may not hold the key to anything more than a perfect day spent in perfect bliss, something sparked in me. It could just be the lingering hypothermia or the pesky crawdad legs tangled in my matted hair but I think this spark comes from a different place. Maybe the spark comes from my magical pelvic chakra, lighting things up for action. But I think, instead, that it comes from somewhere simple and fantastic like those sewn up soft pieces and the nearly renovated girly bit shop, reminding me that so much good is still in me and it might be time to start sharing it again.

Katie The Tarot Whisperer

At first, Katie looks like the last person I would normally consult with for advice on life. A batik sarong tied snug and tight just above her breasts, enough silver to build a small bridge pushed up in circles around her wrists and the orange henna streaking her frizzy silver locks reminds me of something out of *The Dark Crystal.* But she, Katie the Tarot Whisperer, was there along the entryway to the naked hot springs. I felt pulled to chat with her on my way back into the real world. I had so many questions and I figured her amber necklaces, draped and hanging low in thick strands around her neck, held some sort magic and answers for me. Also, I trusted her eyes.

This is not the first time I have crossed the veil into the land of Hocus Pocus to help determine what next steps to take in this beautiful train wreck I call my life. Of course, psychotherapy is always my first choice, but as my beloved therapist gave me her abracadabra, you're mostly fixed seal of approval and sent me on my way almost a year ago, some dabbling in the ether from time to time helps me get through the indecision I am often gripped by.

And ether, I did enter.

My intent for this past year was to repair some of my faulty inner wiring, to try new things, to have my perspective shift so radically that rainbows would shoot out of unicorn heads and disintegrated the dark clouds that regularly hover in the periphery–if not directly over–my life. I wanted a glimpse at the mysteries of what drives us to slip out of bed and face each day. I wanted to know why I am here. I wanted to know how to make this life better.

Like a New Age Magnum P.I., I sought answers. My experiences weren't exactly the stuff of ***A Fortune Teller Told Me*** or ***Eat, Pray, Have Sex with a Hot Brazilian in Bali.*** I don't have that kind of world travel in my budget just yet. Instead, I climbed to an old grove of oaks with David J of Bauhaus one afternoon and asked him all about spirits and God and what can be found in our hearts. I spent a weekend as an apprentice to a 1960's LSD guru and psychotherapist, exploring my shadow side and discussing the ways in which to come to terms with all that is dark and murky inside of me. I consulted a medicine woman in regards to pains in my chest and she worked her magic, rattling and chanting the spirit of my wounded, dead ex right out of my psychic space. I sent scanned photos of my hands to a palm reader in Australia and read the two-page report over and over and over again, memorizing the clues. I drank enough kombucha to rebalance the friendly flora of an entire village to see if I could get drunk or have visions only to pee a lot instead. I was fed psychedelics, wrapped in angora and held like a baby as I looked up to the stars and cried. I learned the mating call of my power animal and practiced the loud and frightening and awful-sounding bugling like an insane person before presenting it to the forest. I waited for answers.

And then there was Katie the Tarot Whisperer.

Katie asked me no questions about my life or what it was I sought. She simply instructed me to shuffle the cards and meditate on what my best self was needing in those moments that I sat next to her, naked men cruising past with penises flopping to and fro in the hot August sun, my daughters fully dressed and giggling among dragonflies at a nearby fountain.

As Katie turned the first card up to begin the reading, she let out a sigh that dropped like a large dusty curtain falling across a darkened stage.

Oh great, I thought, *after all of the shit I've been through, I am going to die on my way home today.* I imagined my kids and I careening off a cliff and exploding into a burst of flames at the bottom of the Napa Valley. Our ghosts would clasp hands and swim through the sky to a great big ball of something drifting between the stars. *Oh, the horror! I had so many plans. So. Many. Glorious. Plans.*

Instead, she placed her hand on mine and said, "Wow. The last few years have been full of chaos and pain. Everything has fallen apart."

That's when my sad little inner child broke down and started to cry. Right there in the blistering sun, penises and bare breasts and New Age sighs all around me; Ray Charles' "Hard Times" filling some corner of my inner ear.

She went on to explain all of the things I already knew but had been too distracted to give attention to: I've only lost the things I no longer need–it is good that they are gone, the old friendships and relationships, the old career, the old ways of doing things. Gone. For good. And also, forever.

Katie also told me some things that I had a hard time hearing–that I have a heart built of courage. That I love like a warrior. I thought, *Really? Most people bug the shit out of me. I don't even want to spend time with my friends lately. And I have so much anxiety and I worry about everything, like crashing this borrowed car into the Napa Valley on the way home today.*

And then she smiled and said, "Your career. You are doing what you do because it is wrapped inside of your heart."

There remains, however, a disproportionate amount of fear in me.

Courageous heart. Love and fear.

I thought back to the night a dear, wonderful friend died. We surrounded her bed, hovering in her mother's living room, in the early evening shadow of majestic Mt. Shasta and we smiled and cried and loved our friend as the cancer siphoned the last bits of her glimmer away. Her mother, the strongest of us all, looked on, coaxing her gorgeous daughter away from the pain and into the arms of some giant entity that filled the air around us all. She repeated, over and over: Everything is love, Lydia. Remember, what would you do if you weren't afraid?

My God.

I am such a coward.

There is so *much* to be afraid of.

Like broken hearts and broken spirits and the things those broken things make people do. Like raising daughters in a country where conservative crap-neck jackasses dismiss rape and want to ban abortion and hate poor people and vaginas. Like everyone I love dying. Like succumbing to a permanent madness instead of bouncing between inter-mittent bouts of despair. Like never having a book pub-lished. Like earthquakes and deforestation and racism and homophobia and flesh- eating bacteria and plane crashes and war and poverty and just trying to live and breathe in a world full of contradictions and madness and greed. There is so much to be afraid of.

But Katie the Tarot Whisperer says I've got what it takes. She says my writing and warrior heart are healing me. She says that big things are just within reach and that I can have it all if I keep my focus, if I utilize my fierce, pumping, beating, disgusting and pulsing bloody chunk of a heart.

I suppose sometimes we need to be reminded of the things that are buried so deep inside that we've convinced our-selves they never really existed in the first place. Sometimes it takes an old woman named Katie and her magic amber necklaces to let us know what is true.

Courageous heart. Love and fear.

What would you do if you weren't afraid?

I would do everything.

thanks to: saviors / cheerleaders / inspiration

(an incomplete list, in no particular order, so I'll leave it blank
so I can write you a note)

* SO MANY THANKS *

Dani Burlison has been a staff writer for a Bay Area alt-weekly, a columnist for *McSweeney's Internet Tendency* and a book reviewer for *The Los Angeles Review.* Her writing also appears or is forthcoming in places like *The Chicago Tribune, The Rumpus, Ploughshares, Hip Mama Magazine, Rad Dad, Spirituality & Health Magazine, Shareable, Prick of the Spindle,* and more. She is a Squaw Valley Writers Work- shop and Lit Camp alumna and lives in Northern California, where she slings zines, teaches writing classes and plans adventures with her two daughters. She can be found at www.daniburlison.com